# Enter *the* Dream

## *And Other Essays*

### Neville Goddard

MB

# Contents

# Enter *the* Dream

God only acts and is in existing beings or men. Embracing the fires of experience, God was consumed by the flames, rose from their ashes, and continues to rise as Jesus Christ, or Divine Imagination. Good and evil are not conditions imposed by some benevolent deity, but states the soul must experience in order to surpass them and awaken as God Himself.

Tonight, I will share with you an experience of a friend, a lady who wrote, saying: "In my dream I possessed the power to be anything I wanted to be. The moment I observed the being or thing I became it, felt its emotion, and shared its thoughts and environment. This I did throughout the night and awoke reluctantly because I was so enjoying the experience."

Now let me tell you what Aldous Huxley wrote about his friend, D. H. Lawrence: "To be with Lawrence was an adventure, because he was not of the order of this world, but belonged to another universe. When I was with him and he shared his experiences, I felt that he knew what it was to be a tree, a daisy, a breaking wave, or the mysterious moon itself. He saw things the mortal eye could not see. He was a sensitive, intelligent man who could cook, sew, embroider, and do woodwork to perfection; yet he could sit alone doing nothing and be completely happy. He could put himself into the skin of an animal and describe in the most convincing detail its dim, inhuman thoughts."

I am quite sure my friend never read that letter, but I gave her my immortal eyes. The eye of Imagination is now open in her and she has shared her experience of going from state to state, from things to persons, knowing their feelings and emotions. How is that possible? Because God is the only actor.

Blake makes this statement: "Eternity Exists and All things in Eternity Independent of Creation which was an act of Mercy. By this it will be seen that I do not consider either the Just or the Wicked to be in a Supreme State, but to be every one of them States of the Sleep into which the Soul may fall in its deadly dreams of Good and Evil when it leaves Paradise following the Serpent."

Everything in the world is yourself pushed out. Every animal there can be entered by you, and you can experience its emotion, for that animal is your very self.

You are the animating power of the universe. All things were made by you and without you was not anything made that was made, for you are life itself. This I know from experience. The universe is alive in you. It has no life on the outside. It is yours to animate, to stop, to let go, and stop again. Blake was right when he said: "God only acts and is in existing beings or men," for God is the only actor, acting imaginatively in the human imagination.

While seated here you can see your home in your mind's eye, but it does not have the cubic reality as does this room. But one day you will think of something and see it more vividly than you now see the speaker. You will enter it, not as a shadow, but as a 3-dimensional space. I have sat in a chair or rested on a bed with my eyes closed as in sleep and seen what I could not see if the lids were open. Knowing exactly where I was and what I was doing, I allowed consciousness to follow vision and stepped into that image which closed itself around me as I set out to explore that world.

I now know the truth of Blake's words: "If the Spectre would enter into these images in his Imagination, approaching them on the Fiery Chariot of his Contemplative Thought. If he would make a friend and companion of any one of these images which always intrigues him to leave mortal things as he must know, then will he rise from the dead; then will he meet the Lord in the air and then he will be Happy."

Many times, while sitting in my chair or lying on my bed, my inner eye has opened and I have seen what no mortal eye could see. Then I would enter into the image by allowing my consciousness to move on its fiery chariot of contemplative thought. Clothed as I am, the world calls me Neville; but I - a conscious being - have moved out of this body and into a world which instantly clothed itself around me; and I explored that world, clothed in a body just as solidly real as the one I left on the bed or chair. If anyone had entered the room they would have thought Neville was sleeping; yet I was fully awake, consciously aware of being separated from my external self.

Look at yourself in the mirror and you are seeing the mask God is wearing in this world of death, but you cannot see the immortal you who cannot die. Your friend or relative may appear to die, but he is not that which is put into the furnace and consumed or buried in a grave. He is that which his I AM is conscious of being, exploring other worlds just as real as this until he experiences the mystery of scripture.

You see, God only acts. Sitting in my chair and seeing what I should not see, I acted by consciously entering into the image I was viewing, to discover it was not a flat surface, but a 3-dimensional reality, complete and ready for occupancy.

My friend knows what it is like to become anything that intrigues her, and I am quite sure she never read the letter Huxley wrote of his friend D. H. Lawrence. This is the same Huxley who showed no interest when I tried to tell him of my birth from above, of David and the visions I have shared with you. He liked me as a friend but he had his own limitations, as everyone does. In a certain social world, if you pronounce a certain word differently you are cataloged as one who is not "in," as it were, and Huxley would not listen to my visions because I did not speak as he thought everyone should. I could have told him things beyond the wildest dreams of his friend D. H. Lawrence, but because of his little stumbling block Aldous could not hear my words.

But I tell you who are seated here tonight: you are the only God. You will know this from experience, for the day is coming when - instead of seeing your thoughts in your mind's eye, you will see them 3-dimensionally, just as you are now seeing the speaker. When the eye of imagination opens you will instantly move into the thought, whether it is regarding something that took place ten thousand years ago or exists in what you might think to be the future. I tell you: there is nothing that is not here and now, ready for you to enter and become one with.

One day you will realize, like Blake, that neither the just nor the wicked are supreme states, and you will be able to forgive everyone for what he is doing or has done. You will know that although his action seems horrible, based upon this level, he is expressing a state and must do as the state dictates. Good and evil are simply states of experience through which the soul of Man must pass in order to awaken to the being that he really is. He must embrace the fires of experience and be consumed before he can rise from the ashes to be one with the being who sent him.

I can't tell you the thrill that is in store for you when the eye of imagination opens, for only then will you be actually seeing for the first time. And when the ears are open you will hear what no mortal ear can hear, as you see what no mortal eye can see. A week or so ago I went to an office regarding my Medicare, and I was asked to prove that I would be sixty-five on my next birthday. I knew that at one time I had obtained my baptismal certificate, but I hadn't seen it in years and had no idea where it was. Two nights ago, about 1:30 A.M., my divine brothers said to me: "Your baptismal certificate is in your wallet." I awoke, opened the dresser drawer and there, inside a wallet my wife had given me back in 1938, was the baptismal certificate I had obtained in 1924 when I needed it to go to London during my dancing career. So, I know that when the eye and ear of imagination is open, every desire of the heart will be seen and heard. That is your destiny.

I say: you are God, the only actor in this world. No matter what you imagine, God is acting. He is the only actor, acting by imagining. You can imagine anything, cover the act with faith by believing in its reality, and it will come to pass. When Blake spoke of eternity in his statement: "Eternity exists and all things in Eternity, independent of creation which was an act of mercy," he was referring to the little garment of flesh and blood you wear. Your garment is. It is eternal. It is a garment that anyone can - and many will - wear. In my case, this is a garment in which one awakes. I am not the garment called Neville, any more than I am any part I ever played on Broadway. I was in six plays but I never was the characters I played there, but simply the actor. And so it is with God. He is the only actor in eternity and God is the human imagination. It is the human imagination who plotted the entire play before he came down and assumed these eternal bodies of limitation and death. And it is the human imagination who will rise from these eternal bodies into Divine Imagination from whence he came.

In the Book of Genesis we are told: "The serpent spoke and said to the woman, 'You will not die for God knows that when you eat of the tree of knowledge of good and evil, your eye will open and you will be like God, knowing good and evil.'" This is something you must know in order to surpass and rise beyond it as Divine Imagination. The serpent knew that as you ate of the fruit of the tree of good and evil, although you would not die, you would embrace the fire of experience, be consumed as its victim, and rise from its ashes as God Himself. That is the story of scripture.

Blake added this wonderful thought, saying that we left paradise following the serpent. This implies that we did not begin here on earth, but left paradise following the serpent of generation who told us that when we embraced the great experience of good and evil we would be consumed in its fire and yet not die, but would rise from it. In his book, John tells it in a lovely way as: "I came out from the Father and came into the world. Again, I am leaving the world and returning to the Father." So, we did not begin here, but - coming out from the Father - we found these garments that seemed to begin in time, but really are an eternal part of the structure of the universe. In my own case this little garment seemed to begin in 1905, but it was always so. It was always growing into manhood and departing in its sixties. Always appearing, occupied by God, moving towards a certain point and then disappearing.

All of these are but garments to be picked up and worn. People think they are the garments they wear. That is because they do not know who God is, for he is in the one who is wearing the garment. It is God, your own wonderful human imagination, who acts and is in existing beings or men. There is no other God, no other actor in the universe.

If you want to test God, you may. Your immortal eyes and ears need not be open to test your creative power. Simply assume you are the one you want to be. Remain faithful to your assumption and, although everything denies it, you will become it. It does not matter who you are or what the world thinks of you; anything is possible to the "I" of imagination. As I mentioned earlier, had Aldous only listened to my message, rather than my English, I could have told him things beyond the wildest dreams of D. H. Lawrence. But I am a Colonial in his eyes and, like all Englishmen; the Colonials are looked down upon. If you don't speak with the Oxford or Cambridge accent, you are a Colonial in their eyes and not one of the boys.

If Aldous had only listened, I could have told him what it was like to not only be the wave, but to be the ocean. When I was but a boy, years before puberty (in fact it stopped at puberty), I would know the night it was going to happen and was afraid to go to sleep. It was marvelous to be the ocean, but to be the breaking wave (a small portion of my being) was frightening. I - the ocean would toss myself - the wave into the skies and then catch myself upon my own bosom as I fell. This experience would happen to me once a month over a period of years. I could have told him what it was like to be infinite light with no circumference, but my accent put barriers in his mind and he could not hear me. This is true the world over.

People judge from appearances, as the individual's true being is unseen by mortal eyes. God comes to us unknown and unseen; but in his own wonderful mysterious manner he lets us discover who he is, and when we do it is in a first person, singular, present tense experience.

I am not trying to flatter you when I tell you that you are God. Everyone is. The one who murders is one with the one who is murdered. The rapist is one with his victim. These are all God's experiences of good and evil in order to surpass good and evil and rise as Divine Imagination who is God Himself. You and I came down and, embracing the fire of experience, we have been consumed by it. Many a time the little garment that we wore turned to ash; and from that ash we found a new body, just like the old one, only new, healthy and wonderful with not a thing missing, to be consumed once more. And we will keep on being consumed, one after the other, until that moment in time when we rise as the Lord Jesus Christ who is God Himself, to be consumed and restored no more. So when Blake said: "God only acts," he really meant it. God not only acts, he is the only actor. When you begin to imagine, God is acting and what you imagine will happen.

I was late getting here tonight. A friend came for lunch yesterday who, knowing the friend who brings me here every week, said: "Isn't he unreliable?" and I immediately answered, "No! Never." She didn't want to hear that and is a very intense lady who knows how to reach him. Today for the first time my friend called to say he couldn't make it. An intense imaginal act produced what the lady wanted to hear, but she will never get the satisfaction of hearing me say he was ever late or did not come.

There are people in this world whose surface veneer appears to be altogether wonderful, but below that surface there is an intensity and they do not know that they are only hurting themselves. She can't touch me, although undoubtedly she has tried; but if she did it would boomerang in a way she would not know. I love her dearly, but she is intense and also of the same school that if you are not of a certain physical background you are not "in."

I have told you unnumbered times that I have no feeling towards any aristocracy in the world. Though I speak of being a descendant of Abraham, it is not after the flesh, but after the spirit; for in the state of Abraham I believed the story that was told me before that the world was. There is no physical aristocracy. Only the aristocracy of the spirit consisting of those who are called and embodied into the body of the Risen Lord. I could tell her this forever and she would not understand. She believes in physical aristocracy, and there is none.

Do not allow anyone to try to impress you with his greatness relative to yours. I have never been able to feel anyone to be my superior. Physically, yes, they can knock me down with one blow. Intellectually, yes - no question about it. Financially, certainly, but I cannot meet anyone that I believe to be my superior. He may be an intellectual giant, a mathematical giant, a musical giant, a giant in a thousand ways, but that does not mean I feel inferior to him.

I was amused today when I looked at my baptismal certificate. My father's occupation was listed as a meat vendor. He had a butcher shop. If this lady had seen that I would no longer be socially acceptable to her. But I urge you to never allow anyone to make you feel less than, because you are infinitely greater than all of the characters of the world put together, as you are God who is playing all the parts. And you will play them all. The phony, and the decent ones, the rich man, the poor man, the known, the unknown - you have played them all or you would not be here. The reason why you are here is because you are on the verge of awakening. And you will awaken from the dream to discover that you created the play, and finding no one to play the parts, you have played them yourself. And when you have played them all, you will awaken by a certain, definite series of events that take place within you. Then the inner eye and ear will open as mine did this morning, when the brothers told me where to find my baptismal certificate. I do not think I have looked in that wallet for thirty years. I do not carry a wallet. I do not drive and my wife carries the money and gives me whatever money I want, so what would I do with a wallet? Yet the crumpled little yellow page was there, just as my brothers said it would be.

I tell you: there isn't a thing that does not exist now and here. We speak of the moon as billions of years old; but you cannot measure your age because there never was a time when you were not, nor will there ever be a time when you will cease to be. You didn't begin in time. You came down into time - which you, yourself created - to experience good and evil, to expand the being that you always were. Even though your birth certificate shows you began in time, you didn't, for you are the wearer of the garment. You are its actor who is God Himself. You cannot even say God is near, because nearness implies separation. He is not near, for when you say, "I am" you are proclaiming he is your very self.

Begin now to believe in your true Being who is God, and whatever you imagine to be so, firmly believe it is so, and it will be so.

Now let us go into the silence.

# Creation - Faith

The mystery of creation is to be understood in terms of faith, so what is faith? It is the assurance of things hoped for, the conviction of things not seen with the mortal eye. Through faith we understand that the world was created by the word of God, so that what is seen was made out of things which do not appear.

"Many suppose that before creation, all was solitude and chaos. That is the most pernicious idea that can enter the mind of man, for it robs the Bible of all sublimity and the nature of the man who entertains that idea a little grubbing worm outside of himself. Eternity exists and all things in eternity, independent of creation which was an act of mercy."[1]

All things exist, and the mystery of their creation must be understood in terms of faith. But faith does not give reality to that which is unseen. Faith is loyalty to the unseen reality! Only in this sense can the meaning of faith be understood.

If you have a goal, although it is unseen, it already exists. Your normal mortal eye cannot see it, but by rearranging the structure of your mind, you can see it clearly. If, as the days follow one another, you remain loyal to this unseen reality, and your goal is reached, you will have discovered the mystery of creation.

Eternity exists and all things in eternity independent of your creative act. You may continue to build only upon what your mortal eye sees, and perpetuate the same thing over and over again, remaining forever where you are. But if you know that all things exist, though unseen at the moment, and you have access to them through your imagination, you can rearrange the pattern of your thinking and change your world by remaining loyal to your unseen construction. And when it externalizes itself by becoming a fact that you may share with others, then you will have found the secret of creation, which was an act of faith.

The 11th chapter of the Book of Hebrews tells fantastic stories of what the ancients performed - and they did everything! Beginning with

---

[1] *William Blake -*

Enoch, all of the characters are named, as well as their achievements. Then it is said: "They received the promises, but not the promise."

Having been promised that if they could believe, it would come to pass, they believed and received the promises. But no one knew the fulfillment of the promise until it broke through in one. Then he knew that by the same act of faith, he could leave this sphere and enter the heavenly one.

God's promise has fulfilled itself in me. I have recorded it for posterity as vividly and as accurately as I can in my book, Resurrection. You can read of my experiences and believe them or disbelieve them. It's up to you. Perhaps at the present time you do not want to leave this sphere and enter the kingdom of heaven.

Now, "By faith we understand that the world was created by the word of God," which is His power and wisdom, called Christ. Any Christ other than he who is crucified, buried, and rises in you, is false. And anyone who teaches of an outside Christ is a false teacher.

Paul tells us: "The mystery hidden from the ages, Christ in you, is the hope of glory." Any hope you have of entering a glory that transcends all earthly power and wisdom is already in you, but hidden. Christ is the way, the pattern to follow for entrance into that glory.

If everything exists, whether visible or invisible, then my father and mother who have departed this world exist, and would revel in anything that I accomplish here. Although my mother left this world in 1941 and my father in `59, I can bring them into my mind's eye and hear them speak of their pride in their son. Believing that everything I can conceive is part of the structure of the universe, I can assume they are fully aware of my accomplishments, so I listen to their joy.

Now, can I remain faithful to that scene? My faith is not going to give it reality, but my loyalty to the unseen reality will. I listen and remember what I heard, and in the tomorrows I continue to remember. Then, in its own appointed time, when that which I have been faithful to externalizes itself, I will have found the great secret of creation.

God tells us he does not create something out of nothing, for all things are! That he calls a thing that is not now seen as though it were seen, and the unseen becomes seen.[2] Instead of calling something out of nothing,

---

[2] *Romans 4:17*

you simply rearrange that which already is until it implies what you want. Then you remain loyal to that unseen reality.

Faith contains a power which can link you to a world where you are eternal. Paul tells us to put our faith, not in the works of men, but in the power of God. And no earthly power - be it atomic, megatons of multi-megatons - can compare to that power!

Can you conceive of being a power so great that if you desire, you can stop the world? That you can make it stand still and see it as dead? Then release it and let the world continue to fulfill its so-called intentions?

Could you deal with such a power by changing your intentions, thus causing the world to be reanimated and do the opposite? That is the power which will be yours when you know you are one with the body of love, called the Everlasting Savior.

Contemplate this thought. On this level you may achieve any objective, and prove to yourself that invisible states, when properly rearranged, will externalize what they imply, for the potency of every imaginal act is in its implication.

Listen closely to your invisible thoughts. What do you hear? What are your words implying? That is their potency. What do you want? Name it and rearrange the structure of your mind to imply you no longer desire it, because you already have it!

Perhaps another has injured you or caused you grief. It doesn't matter what has been done, when you know this law you can forgive anyone by rearranging the structure of your mind and set him free by imagining it never happened!

You see, there are two things that displease God. One is the lack of faith in "I am he", and the other is eating of the tree of knowledge of good and evil by using yourself as the criteria as to what is good and what is evil. Unless you believe you are the seeming other who caused your grief, you will continue to reproduce the same unhappiness and miss your mark in life by dying in your sins. So, without faith it is impossible to please yourself!

For the moment, think of everything as existing now! Although unseen by your mortal mind, your desire exists and can be seen in your imagination. Although your father and mother may be unseen by the world, they exist, and the love they have for you has never passed away.

Because all things are, you may use them or those who are now in your world.

If, for instance, your friends heard of your good fortune, would they empathize with you or be envious? Do not choose one who would sympathize with you, for you do not want sympathy. You either want empathy or envy. If you know someone who, when hearing of your good fortune would now go wild with envy, use her. Or, if you know one who would rejoice because of your good fortune, take that image.

It's your choice, but you must remain loyal to the unseen reality you have constructed. Your faith will not give it reality, for faith is your loyalty to the unseen reality. "Abraham believed, and it was accounted unto him for righteousness," and all things come out of Abraham.

Someone once defined faith as:

> *Believing what is incredible,*
> *Or it is no virtue at all.*
>
> *Hope is hoping when things are hopeless,*
> *Or it is no virtue at all.*
>
> *And love is forgiving what is unforgivable,*
> *Or it is no virtue at all.*

These are the three virtues under which the civilized world comes - Faith, Hope and Love.

You may not be able to see the fulfillment of your desires with your mortal eye. Your senses and reason may deny their existence, but this is the way God created the world. You are invited to imitate him as a dear child, by remaining faithful to the unseen reality in your mind until it becomes seen in your world. And when it does you will have proved God's law.

Then that great moment will come when that which was promised in the beginning erupts, and the creative power you once knew yourself to be is restored, only magnified because of your journey into this world of death.

All of the promises of God have found their Yes in me. I remain with you now only to encourage you to move into an entirely different awareness. There is nothing here, however, to aid you concerning that world. How can you understand God's power, when you only know the power to burn wood and boil water? You are aware that a bomb can kill millions; yet you also know that the ones who created and dropped the bomb will die, just like the millions killed; so you have nothing to compare to the power of that world, as it transcends anything known to man.

I have described the pattern for entrance into that world. It consists of a series of four mystical events which, when experienced, frees the individual from this level and opens the door into the world of the promise. I have shared my experiences; yet men - believing I am Neville who will die as everyone does here - do not believe they are the Messiah which is to come, so they turn a deaf ear in my direction.

But I will continue to share my experiences and leave them behind in my books, just as Paul did in the form of letters, and those who experienced the visions recorded the gospels. Those who wrote the gospels knew what they had experienced; but man has misinterpreted the message, believing Jesus Christ is external to self and not realizing he is God's creative power and wisdom.

My visions have paralleled those recorded in the Book of Luke. Luke does not claim that his experiences were chronologically accurate, but that he feels better qualified to write the source material. I have told it chronologically, just as it happened to me.

Now I tell you this: As persons differ, so will the experiences. Two people here have had that birth. In one case there was no witness; therefore, his witness is scripture. In the other case, the lady had three witnesses: two brothers and a friend she thinks of as a brother. So, because we do differ in the kingdom, the visions will differ, but the pattern will remain the same.

Even if you haven't had the experiences, you can construct a scene that would imply scripture has been fulfilled in you. Wouldn't it be wonderful if you could say to your closest friend, or most bitter opponent, "There is no doubt in my mind that I have been born from above, for I have held that infant wrapped in swaddling clothes in my hands." How would you feel if that were true? What scene would you construct? Remember, all things exist.

Scripture exists, so use it to construct your scene. It is said that three men were present at the birth. Church tradition claims the three kings were brothers; but friends may be used as witnesses, as the scene you are creating is for the purpose of implication, for therein contains the power. But one must lift the child and place him in your arms.

Imagine, and then watch the mystery of creation unfold in terms of faith, by remaining loyal to the unseen reality of that which already exists. "Unto you is born this day a Savior..." And the only Savior is the Lord God! The infant wrapped in swaddling clothes is only a sign, given to tell you that what I have told you is true. Imagine anything that would imply God's birth has already happened. Remain faithful to that scene, and when it happens there will be no uncertainty on your part.

Salvation history is over! We are not here to sow, for the fields are already white with harvest. Because all things are, and the harvest is, you are not here to till the soil and plant the seed, but to reap that which you did not sow. If you know that faith is simply loyalty to unseen reality, you can construct a scene, remain loyal to it and harvest it, for everything is already completed.

God conceived the history of salvation, plotted it, and fulfilled it by becoming humanity. Believing that he already did accomplish his purpose, humanity is raised to enter the kingdom once more and God's second coming has been fulfilled.

But until individual man believes in his own wonderful human imagination, God remains imprisoned within him. If you do not harvest God's promise it is only because you do not believe!

Now I want to share a dream of a friend, as it contains a message for us all. Bear in mind that the dreamer is protean. Like the legendary god, Proteus, who served Neptune and would assume any shape or form in his service, God is the dreamer in you and assumes the forms of all the characters in your dream.

In this lady's dream she encounters her mother, yet knows she is herself. Her husband, yet her father, was missing, and her mother said: "Listen, I can hear his voice." Then the scene changed, and she and her mother are being entertained by four little men, each one foot high. As she looked into the eyes of one of them, she realized he was her father. Calling her mother's attention to this fact, her mother approached, touched him and said something in code. Then suddenly she knew that her father was not free to identify himself and she awoke sobbing.

This dream speaks volumes. Remember, all dreams are egocentric, with God as the dreamer. Everyone is seeking the Father, the cause of the phenomena of life, not realizing he is imprisoned in all. Belief, however, will set him free! If you will imagine David standing before you and feel the Father/Son relationship. Remain loyal to that scene, you will release your heavenly Father!

Because of one's former religious training, when the truth is heard that will set him free, he is torn between the two. To think that one can come to hear my message, yet still believe in what the churches teach, is like what someone once said to me: "I have given up all belief in numerology and astrology, but the moon is passing Venus tonight and because he is in my second house I know what to expect tomorrow." They have completely given up their belief BUT... That big "BUT" happens in all.

This lady's vision was so clear. Her father, entertaining in a group of four and not free to come forward and identify himself, is the four-faced man Ezekiel speaks of. In his vision every living creature had four faces. Beside each creature was a wheel, with wheels within, all moving in the same direction.

This has been a perfect revelation to her, if she will accept it, telling her she is either for me or against me. Would that you be either hot or cold - believing my words or leaving, never to have anything to do with me again - rather than being lukewarm and remaining on the fence, warmed by my words, but unwilling to put them to use in the form of belief.

I have had people say: "I'll come hear you. You are interesting, but I know that in order to get ahead in life I must know the right people and be at the right place at the right time. That is the reality to which I choose to anchor myself." This is what her wonderful vision disclosed to me.

Another lady wrote, sharing a very long dream filled with scriptural symbology. The crystal-clear water rising. Logs cut to the height of men who were carrying them vertically. A dog with a human face. A piece of rope becoming animated and acting like a serpent, entangling the little dog. Each symbol was perfect, and when properly arranged reveals the mystery of salvation. The wood is the spinal cord upon which God is crucified as Man. Caleb, the symbol of faith wears a human face, dies only for a moment, for faith is destined to be freed.

Another lady wrote, saying: "I woke laughing, hearing these words, 'It's so easy to know you are God. All you need to do is to expand.' "This is true. William Blake began his great poem, "Jerusalem," on the sixth line, saying: "Awake! Awake O sleeper of the land of shadows, wake! Expand! I am in you and you in me, mutual in love divine." Love's secret is expansion. Contract your senses and you see multitudes. Expand them and you will see one Man, one Love!

Dwell upon this great mystery of creation in terms of faith. All ministers, rabbis, and preachers teach faith - but faith in what? In little icons? A lighted candle? Our maid comes every Monday and we always give her our used candles. This afternoon we gave her two, which she will take to her church to light. She has faith in a discarded, lighted candle!

All of these things are on the outside. Faith in any power other than He who is within you is false, and anyone who teaches a power on the outside is a false teacher. Christ in you is your hope of glory, and there is no other power.

The world was constructed in the mind's eye, out of things unseen by the mortal eye, and made alive by faith. Eternity exists and all things in eternity, independent of the creative act, which is the assumption of unseen reality and loyalty to its assemblage.

In spite of denial by your senses and reason, if you will be faithful to your unseen assumption, it will externalize itself. That is how all worlds come into being, but men do not understand this. Structuring their world based upon the evidence of their senses, they continue to perpetuate that which they do not desire.

Knowing what you want, close your eyes and enter its fulfillment, knowing that God is seeing what you are seeing. That He is hearing what you are saying; and what God sees and hears and remains loyal to, He externalizes.

Now let us go into the silence.

# Divine Signs

Those raised in the Christian or Jewish faith are taught to believe that scripture is secular history. But I know that the story of Jesus, from his conception by the Holy Spirit to his ascension into heaven, is a sign rendered by God to those who will receive it.

The visions of the Old and New Testament are unchanged, eternal realities, which are forever. One day you will encounter what appears on paper to be a person, but he will be a state of consciousness, personified.

When Paul recognized this truth he said: "From now on I regard no one from a human point of view. Even though I once regarded Christ from a human point of view, I regard him thus no longer." After the revelation Paul realized that Jesus Christ was the creative power and wisdom of God, and not a person as he had been taught. But because God became Man that Man may become God, every attribute of God - whether it be faith, called Abraham, or the power and wisdom of God, called Jesus Christ - was personified.

Although addressing the Corinthians, Paul was speaking of the characters in scripture when he said: "From now on I regard no one from the human point of view." No longer able to think of Abraham as a person, as you are a person, Paul tells this story: "It is written in scripture that Abraham had two sons. One born of a slave according to the flesh, and the other born according to the promise." Here Paul is telling you that by your physical birth you are that one born according to the flesh. But Abraham's second son is born of a free woman, born according to the promise.

Then Paul explains the allegory of the two sons, telling us that Hagar - a servant of Sarah - was given over to Abraham, who sired the child Ishmael.[3] Isn't that this world? As an offspring of the slave, Hagar, we struggle to make a living, to pay rent and taxes, always trying to keep ourselves above the flood of illusion.

---

[3] *Meaning: "His hand is against every man, and every man's hand is against him"*

But after the vision Paul realized that there is another birth, which takes place within. Called Isaac, that second son comes from Sarah, for he is born according to the promise. This is all symbolism, for when your spiritual birth occurs a child wrapped in swaddling clothes will appear to symbolize your birth. There are two distinct births from two distinct beings. One from the womb of woman[4] and the other from the skull of generic man, called Sarah. Having seen the vision and, understanding its message, Paul no longer thought of Abraham, Isaac, Jacob - or any character of scripture, including Jesus Christ - as human. Even though he formerly thought of them that way and heard their story as secular history, he regarded them thus no longer.

In his 3rd chapter to the Ephesians, Paul makes this statement: "When you read the Old Testament, you will perceive my insight into the mystery of Christ, which was not made known to men in other generations, but is now revealed to his holy apostles and prophets through the Spirit." It was not known prior to its revelation in Paul that the mystery of Christ comes from within!

In the same letter to the Ephesians, Paul speaks of himself and those with whom he shared the vision, saying: "It has been shown us the mystery of his will according to his purpose which he set forth as a plan in Christ, for the fullness of time." To Paul, Christ - God's power and wisdom - is a plan of redemption, which is crucified on humanity and will be raised from the dead.

I tell you now: he has made known unto me the sacred secret of his will according to his purpose, which he set forth in Christ as a plan for the fullness of time. And when that time is fulfilled, he who is buried in you will erupt and God's purpose will be revealed.

The revelation of purpose gives everything meaning. You could have a million dollars and die tomorrow. Those who inherit your estate will give you lip service, but even after one generation the caring will cease and within three generations they will forget you. That is this world, but there is a plan buried in you which reveals God's purpose and gives meaning to all life! When that plan is unveiled in you, you will know why you do what you do and dream what you dream. You will know why you

---

[4] *Hagar*

have certain visions. You will realize that everything contains within itself a symbolic significance. I will show you in a very simple way.

Tonight, you may dream that you have an intimate relationship with another. Upon awakening, ask yourself what the one you encountered represents to you, and a wonderful answer will come from the depth of your soul. You will discover that, on a certain level, they represent a glorious state.

For instance: I know a brilliant man who graduated from Yale at the age of 19 and remained there for many years to teach higher mathematics. As an American of many generations, he once said to me: "We should have only English-speaking people in the world," and he meant it. He was a very positive, brilliant person. If in dream you should see this man in a relationship, upon awakening you would realize he represents something positive, strong, and intellectual. Then watch, for whether one knows of the events or not, soon thereafter the one impregnated will be inspired to do something creative; for God is a creator who goes about creating, and you saw God's creative act.

On this level you may think this is sordid, but that is because you do not know God's symbolism. Speaking to everyone in the language of symbolism, that which the world may condemn is a glorious act of God.

God, being protean, plays all the parts. Wearing the garment of another, you see an act which could be a horrible one, based upon your concept of that individual. But if it is a lovely act, a glorious child - such as a poem, painting, or a design for a new home - will appear out of that union. That's all the experience means; but man is so rooted in the flesh, he gives it a Caesar's concept, which blinds him to God's symbolism.

You may or may not believe me, but the story of Jesus - from his conception by the Holy Spirit to his ascension into heaven - is simply a sign rendered by God to those who will receive it.

I have fulfilled scripture. There are those who will accept my message, and those who will not. If you who believe my word and ever see me in vision in the creative act, it is because I am fertilizing the story of the gospel in you. I am the father of that which is being fertilized.

I refer you, now to the 4th chapter of 1 Corinthians, where Paul speaks, saying: "You have unnumbered guides in Christ, but not many fathers. I became your father in Christ."

This is a mystery. Unnumbered people will tell you about Christ, based upon theory and speculation but not from experience. The King James Version calls these men instructors. Paul is saying that although there are many instructors, after his experiences are accepted he sires them.

Paul shared his vision, saying: "When it pleased God to reveal his son in me, I conferred not with flesh and blood." To whom could one turn after having experienced the vision of God's son calling him father? How could anyone tell you anything about a vision you have had? God's son revealed himself in me, and as I tell it I draw those who will believe me. Although they may not understand, they will modify their preconceived concepts of the Christian faith to conform to what I have experienced. The union will occur and that concept will unfold within them.

God, being protean, uses Neville (or anyone who has unfolded the pattern within himself) and wearing that mask he has union with one who has accepted the story of salvation. Then, having fertilized, it the pattern unfolds within him.

In 1929 I had union with the Risen Lord, and 30 years later, in 1959, I was born from above. If the part you are predestined to play in the body of God calls for a shorter interval, your birth may happen sooner; but my part has been a complete unfoldment of scripture, and it has taken 30 years.

We are told that when Jesus began his ministry he was about thirty years of age. This does not mean thirty years after a physical birth, but thirty years after the spiritual union. When your spiritual birth will take place only the Father knows; but we are told in the Book of Habakkuk: "Every vision has its own appointed hour. It ripens, it will flower. If it be long, wait, for it is sure and it will not be late."

Paul tells us there are eight levels of the body of God: the apostles, prophets, teachers, workers of miracles, and so on. If you are destined to play other than that of the apostle, then maybe the latent time between union and birth of that particular part is not the same.

There is no dream, no vision, without meaning, for God speaks to man through the medium of dream and unveils himself in a vision. What you experience in vision is right for that particular level of your being, but when it is reduced to this level the thought would be totally wrong. Man, having eaten of the tree of knowledge of good and evil, decides what is right and what is wrong, thereby descending into the mire of confusion. But when he turns around he discovers that nothing is either right or wrong. On a certain level it is right and, on another level, it is wrong. So, learn to accept every level, and as you do you will ascend the tree of life to discover that every level - when viewed from there - is right when you know how to interpret it.

He has made known unto me the mystery of his sacred will according to his purpose, which he set forth as a plan in Christ for the fullness of time. I now know that Christ is not a person, and regard no scriptural character from the human point of view, but rather a state of consciousness personified. I once regarded Christ from the human point of view, but now I see him as the creative power of imagination and the wisdom of imagination, with a plan buried in that power.

I now know I am the cross God's power wears as His plan of salvation has unfolded in me. He awoke and resurrected himself in me, and the entire story of Jesus Christ unfolded and revealed me as God the Father.

I have told you my experiences. If the world will not believe me it really doesn't matter, for I will find my remnant - my ten per cent - who will believe my story in spite of what they formerly believed. In this audience there are those who, although they attend regularly, continue to bring their barriers with them and will not accept my story. Others, bringing their preconceived misconceptions of scripture with them, depart never to return.

A friend brought a lovely lady to the last lecture, at which time she told me she would take my theories under consideration. I told her they were not theories, that I speak from experience. Then she said: "But I am an ordained minister," and I replied: "That means nothing to me. Have you had the vision of Christ? Did the one who ordained you have the vision of Christ? If not, it's the blind leading the blind."

"You can't take my theories under consideration, only what I have experienced. If it does not fit your prefabricated misconception of scripture, all well and good, but I am sharing my visions, my experiences. They are all revelations, not theory." She was very sweet, and left saying that this was her first lecture.

You don't come for one time, and hear something so radically different from what you have been trained to believe and expect to swallow it hook, line, and sinker. I would ask my friend to loan her my book, Resurrection, and have her read the chapter on resurrection. It's all documented.

I have referenced the Old Testament and - like Paul - ask you to keep my interpretation of the Old Testament in mind as you read my experiences. If so, you will find light coming from what you did not formerly understand, for the pattern has awakened in me. The New Testament is the fulfillment of the Old. It's not the other way around. The pattern, the mystery of his will, remains sealed in the Old Testament until the fullness of time, when the seal is broken and individual man resurrects, fulfilling scripture.

If you test your creative power on this level, the statement: "Whatsoever you desire, believe you have received it and you will," will no longer be a great theory given lip service, but will be known from experience. Believe you are the man (or woman) you want to be. Catch the feeling that you have already arrived. Look at your world from that assumption, knowing its truth.

Now, believe your assumption has its own appointed hour to flower. Persist in your belief and no power on earth can stop it from hardening into fact. This is Christianity!

There is no limit to your creative power. The most horrible problem will be resolved if you will but conceive a solution in your mind's eye. Anyone can do it. It doesn't take an Einstein to imagine a problem is resolved. Do not limit your creative power by determining the ways and means for it to come about, for imagination has at its disposal ways that are past finding out.

Do not be concerned as to how, when, or where - only the end. If you are in debt, what is the solution? That you win the lottery or an uncle dies and leaves you his fortune? No! The end is that you are debt-free. How would you feel if all of your bills were paid? Assume that feeling and let imagination harden that feeling into a fact!

Every problem has a solution. Imagine the solution and assume it is true. What would you see and do were it true? How would you feel? Persist in that feeling and in a way no one knows the solution will come to pass.

There is nothing impossible to God, and God is crucified on you as your own wonderful human imagination! There never was another and there never will be another God, and all things are possible to him. If you can imagine the end, knowing all things are possible to imagination and remain faithful to that assumption as though it were true, imagination will harden into fact.

Remember, creative power will not operate itself. Knowing what to do is not enough. You, imagination's operant power, must be willing to assume that things are as you desire them to be before they can ever come to pass.

Now, let us return to the divine signs. The Bible begins with the story of Abraham, which is an allegory - a story told as if true - leaving the one who reads it to discover its fictitious character and learn its lesson. If the story of Abraham, Sarah, and their offspring Isaac, as well as the story of Abraham, Hagar and their offspring, Ishmael, are allegories, and Abraham is the father of us all - where is the reality of the story?

The New Testament begins: "This is the genealogy of Jesus Christ the son of David, the son of Abraham. Abraham begot Isaac and Isaac begot Jacob and Jacob begot Judas and his brother." If Abraham, the source of all life, is an allegory, then everything is an allegory, including Jesus Christ; for he is the culmination of the entire genealogy that begins in the first chapter of Matthew. Search and you will discover that scripture is a wonderful plan of salvation buried in Christ, God's creative power and wisdom, who is crucified on man as his own wonderful human imagination. Knowing that the plan is contained in you, belief will awaken it.

You may be completely unaware of the moment the plan was fertilized; but it must and will be fertilized by one who has awakened from the dream of life, for the plan that is to be born is spirit. One who has not yet awakened can be used to bring about a beautiful poem, a play, or a wonderful story on this level; but God's plan of salvation can only be fertilized by one who has already been raised from the dead, and God - being protean - will assume that mask to play that part.

Now let us go into the silence.

# Election *and* Change
## *of* Consciousness

Election is an act of God, not based upon any inherent superiority of those elected, but grounded in the love and grace of God and in his promises to the Father. Let no one boast who is called. Let no one boast who is elected, for all will be called, but in God's own predetermined time. So tonight, my subject is "Election and Change of Consciousness".

God speaks to Man through the medium of dream and reveals himself in vision, and we are past masters of misinterpreting his words. A dream is a parable containing a single jet of truth. Don't try to give meaning to every word or event of the dream. Perhaps there will be several dreams, several stories in a single dream - then each story contains its own jet of truth. Let me share one such dream of a friend. Her dream is in three parts. It is a wonderful dream on the higher level.

The lady states: "I found myself in an old, comfortable farmhouse. Outside an old horse grazed in the sun and an old dog slept under a tree. Suddenly a man appeared at my door and said: 'You have been chosen and must leave this place.' For a moment I panicked. What would I do about the house and the animals outside? Perhaps I could sell them or give them away. Then the man, having read my thoughts, said: 'No, you cannot sell them or give them away. You must leave them as they are, and your leaving must be voluntary.'

The moment I chose to leave, the scene changed and I am in an entirely different world, talking to a man and a woman. They tell me that I must play three games, of which two have been completed, although I couldn't remember playing them. Now standing in the center of a beautiful green field, I see an enormous mountain in the distance. I am told that I must run across this field, gather anything I can along the way, and reach the top of the mountain in ten seconds. Then I must interpret what I have accomplished along the way. Scooping up a few stones, I began to run, stopping occasionally to gather more stones along the way. When I reached the top of the mountain I discovered my stones had become golden nuggets which had fused together. Extending my hand for those who were there to see, I said: 'This is my mind of golden wisdom' and they replied: 'You have found the way.'

Then the dream changed and I am standing gazing at a child lying in a crib. Its head appeared to be indented, as though it had been lying on rocks or sand. Rubbing the child's head, I smoothed its skin and it smiled. Then I dressed it, made it more comfortable, and as I was feeding it I awoke, still seeing the smile on its face."

God spoke to this lady in a glorious dream. A house is the symbol of the state from which you abide. Hers was very comfortable. A dog is the symbol of faith. Called Caleb, in scripture, he is the one who crossed the river with Joshua. He is called the hound of faith. Now, a horse is the symbol of the mind. In her case he represented a comfortable way of thinking.

Then the man appears to tell her she is chosen.[5] So the Lord appeared, not as some strange creature from outer space or as an impersonal force, but as an ordinary man. He tells her she is chosen. Chosen to leave this age. She cannot sell or give her present state of consciousness away. She must voluntarily leave it for another to occupy.

Entering an entirely different age, she meets two, and there is conflict until she reaches the mountain top where the God in her reveals the mind of golden wisdom. Now, in Paul's last letter to Timothy, he says: "The time of my departure has come." Then he mentions three events, saying: "I have fought the good fight. I have finished the race. I have kept the faith." Like Paul, she has fought the good fight and finished the race, for she has kept the faith - just as everyone will - for it's God who is doing it all.

Then she finds wisdom, personified as a little child, he who said: "Before he created the heavens I stood beside him as a little child. I was daily his delight, rejoicing constantly before him and delighting in the affairs of men. Listen to me carefully. He who finds me finds life. He who misses me injures himself. He who hates me, loves death." She found the child. She found life. Animating bodies in this world of death, we are destined to become life-giving spirits by finding life. Having won the

---

[5] *In scripture, God's messenger is always the Lord himself, for "my name is in him" -*

race, having kept the faith, having fought the good fight, she has found the child. Don't be concerned about all the little pieces of a dream; simply see the symbols present there.

Now let me repeat once again: Scripture is not history, and the characters depicted there are not persons, but personifications of eternal states of consciousness. We all started this journey into death in the state of Abraham. In the 23rd chapter of Genesis it is said that Sarah dies and Abraham becomes a sojourner in a strange land for 400 years. Called the father of the multitude, God promised Abraham that he would return, bringing all with him. Going to the Hittites, Abraham tells them he has no land to bury his wife, and they say: "Hear us, my lord; you are a mighty prince among us. Take the choicest of our sepulchers; none will withhold his sepulcher from you, or hinder you from burying your dead."

May I tell you: every child born of woman is God the Father, buried in the sepulcher of the Hittites, called Canaanites. Every black man, every white man, every nationality, race or creed born of woman, is a Canaanite where God the Father is buried. This was a deliberate act, not a punishment. Listen to the words in the 82nd Psalm: "God has taken his place in the divine council where he holds judgment saying: 'You are gods, sons of the Most High, all of you; nevertheless, you will die like men and fall as one man, O princes.'" We are the ones who deliberately fell into these garments, these sepulchers. A god is entombed in every skull. You didn't begin in your mother's womb. You are buried in the body your mother wove for you, and from that sepulcher you will be called in fulfillment of God's promise.

So let me repeat: Election is an act of God, not based on any inherent superiority of those elected, but grounded in the love and the grace of God and in his promises to the Father. It is to the Father that the promise is made. Everyone has been promised that he will die and will be raised from that state. Everyone will be called from the age of death to once again enter the age of everlasting life. This lady has been called. She has been chosen and all the events recorded in scripture will take place in her.

It thrills me beyond measure to know that in this small circle so many are being called. Everyone will be called, for God is in them and God cannot fail to lift himself up in everyone. Having played all the states, as everyone must, you will have kept the faith and God will keep his promise and lift himself up, in you, just as he laid himself down in you.

It is the God in you who said: "No one takes my life, I lay it down myself. I have the power to lay it down and the power to lift it up again." As God's power is lifted up in you, you depart this age.

Now, in another's dream, he is driving his wife's car over a mountainous road. Suddenly the hair on the back of his head catches fire and he turns and rubs his head against the back of the seat to put out the fire. But in so doing, he loses control of the car and it goes over the cliff in slow motion. Seeing that the fall is about 300 feet, he opens the door of the car and jumps, saying to himself "This is a dream. I AM!" With that thought in mind he descends to the ground below as light and softly as a flake of snow, and awakes on his bed, saying to himself: "I have had this dream three times, and each time I have written it to Neville, but this is the first time I have awakened in the dream."

What is the single jet of truth in this dream? He is riding in his wife's car. A wife is that to which I AM [is] attached. A state which bears my name. There are infinite states in this world and when you enter a state you are wedded to it. The state may be one of luxury or ill health, the state of being ignored or famous; but any state is God's emanation, his wife. The dream denotes a departure from the state in which the God in him has been residing, into an entirely different state. Perhaps he is presently wedded to a state in which he is making $10,000 a year and he desires to live in the state of earning $40,000 or even $100,000. There's nothing wrong with that. Every state is a garment, ready and waiting for you to slip on, and you're free to wear - and thereby marry - any state you like.

If you want to be important in the eyes of shadows, you can; but when the God in you awakes all the shadows will vanish and you will return enhanced and glorified to the being that you were prior to your descent into death, for this is the world of death. Everything here appears, it waxes, it wanes, and it vanishes. You do not die when men call you dead. You are still clothed in the same garment, but younger than you were when you made your exit, to again wax, wane, and vanish, to repeat the act over and over again. This is what the Bible teaches. Read the 20th chapter of the Book of Luke: "The sons of this age marry and are given in marriage; but those who are accounted worthy to attain to that age neither marry nor are given in marriage, for they cannot die anymore."

There are two distinct ages. We remain in this age, experiencing states over and over again until we are elected and called to enter that age. And because you are so unique you are called one by one, for no one can take your place. You are a part of the body of God, the God who deliberately fell. The God who, reaching the limit of contraction, buried himself in his chosen sepulcher (your skull), from which he will rise as promised in the beginning. "I say, ye are gods, sons of the Most High, all of you" (not just a few, but all of you). "Nevertheless, you will die like men and fall as one man, O princes." Now I say to you, O mighty princes: the sepulcher you chose was paid for by 400 shekels of silver.[6]

When Abraham entered the sepulcher, becoming a Hittite, God died by completely forgetting who I AM. He didn't pretend, but buried himself in your skull and died, there to remain until I AM born from above. Then memory returns. But until that time, no matter what position he plays in the world, he does not know who he is. You can be the wisest of the wise, the strongest of the strong, and still not know who you are until God awakens in you. "He has taken the foolish to shame the wise. He has taken the weak to shame the strong. He has taken those who are low and despised, even things that are not, to bring to nothing things that are."

Jesus Christ is defined as the power of God and the wisdom of God. "He is our source, having been made our wisdom, our righteousness and our redemption." God's own power is Christ Jesus. His own wisdom is Christ Jesus, and he has made Christ Jesus your wisdom and your redemption; therefore, Christ in you is the hope of glory, for when Christ returns, God has gathered his creative power and wisdom back unto himself - that power and wisdom which was buried in man.

My friend, in her vision, brought her golden nuggets back to the top of the mountain, where all of her experiences in the world of death were gathered together and fused into the one mind of golden wisdom. So God enhances himself; having reached the limit of contraction he expands. Having reached the limit of opacity he becomes translucent; therefore, he is far greater than he was when he fell into the Hittite.

When a little child is born, he lives because God buried himself in him. Do not think that because someone is going to the gas chamber

---

[6] *Four hundred, in Hebrew, carries the sign of the cross. The price God paid to become you -*

tonight he is less than you are. Do not allow anyone to pull his rank on you either, for no one is important in this world. There is no one but God who is buried in every person in the world, and every person is equal. So let me repeat: election is an act of God, not based upon any inherent superiority of those elected, but grounded in the love and grace of God and in his promises to the Father. Everyone was promised that he would be redeemed, and God has kept his promise.

Christ Jesus in me is God's power and wisdom, and when redeemed, I am he, for everything said of him I have experienced. I still wear a garment called Neville, but I have awakened to another age. I am still the same man in the world of Caesar. I still sign my name on my checks, and the shadows who receive them can exchange them for more shadows based on my signature. But the being that is called into an entirely different world was before the beginning, but enhanced now because of the experience. So, everyone is richer for coming into this world, for God's creative power has been enhanced.

The child she saw is a symbol of her transformed creative power. She has experienced a change of age. But the man experienced a change of state. I can tell him tonight that the dream doesn't mean he is departing this world. He has a wife to support and little children to educate. The dream has nothing to do with breaking his neck here, or divorcing his wife, for he is not married to her, but to a state in this world. He leaves a state and enters another - be it noble or ignoble - for he was driving his wife's car when he awoke to realize it was a dream.

Now, in the waking dream you can learn to control your imagination so that you can set in motion your status from one level to another, but you cannot change the age. That comes out of the blue. That comes when you least expect it. No one can earn the exit from this age. That comes upon you suddenly, as promised in the beginning. So let no one boast and tell you they earned the kingdom. We are all put through the furnaces for his own sake, for his name he cannot give to another. It is yours, as promised, before the beginning of the world. "I came out from the Father and came into the world. Again, I am leaving the world and returning to the Father." Here is pre-existence, incarnation, departure, and pre-destination. It takes not just three-score-and-ten, but a long, long while. And the pigment of your skin, your social or intellectual position, has nothing to do with your departure from this age.

If you want the shadow of worldly fame you may have it, but it will not aid you in waking from the dream of life. If you will fall in love with what I am talking about, and set your heart fully upon the grace that is coming to you at the unveiling of Jesus Christ in you, you are on the verge. But if that doesn't interest you, and more money does, then get more money. If you want more cash, more fame, whatever you desire - get them, for they are all shadows. A big home is a big shadow, and a little home a little shadow, so it doesn't really matter.

But tonight, dwell on these two. Like the lady, you cannot earn, any more than she earned it, for she was called. But like the other, you can leave the state to which you are now wedded. How do you do it? By the act of feeling. Feel the tones of reality that would be yours were you wedded to the state of your fulfilled desire. What would the feeling be like were you the person you would like to be? Feeling moves you from one state to another.

Everything is a state which is real, yet invisible. Not knowing this, and seeing no evidence to support your desired state, you may return to the former one. Expecting the new state to happen now, you don't remain faithful to it. But if you will remain there until it becomes natural to think from that state, it will be born in your world. There is a period of time between your entrance into the invisible state and its visibility, and it has to come. Everything has an interval of time. The vision has its own appointed hour. If it seems long, wait. It is sure and it will not be late. A little sheep takes five months, a man nine months, a horse one year. All these are fixed intervals of time.

How long will it take for a state to become objective? As long as it takes the nature of that seed to hatch. All you are called upon to do is to go into the state and remain there psychologically. Although you will continue to physically walk the earth as one person, as you think from your desired psychological state, it takes on physical tones and becomes a fact in your world. This is how you move from state to state as you wait for the promise of God to fulfill itself.

On that day you will be called and incorporated into his immortal body to express a far greater translucency and expansion than you knew prior to the start of your journey into the world of death. I can't tell you the thrill that is in store for you when you experience the embrace of love. There are no words to describe it, but as you embrace, you fuse to become one body, one Spirit, yet without loss of identity. Everyone will be called into that same union. Everyone will experience the end of the journey, for not one will be lost in all my holy mountain.

Now let us go into the silence.

# Esau - Jacob - Israel

We are told by Paul in II Timothy 3:16: "All Scripture is inspired by God and profitable for teaching, for reproof, for correction, and for training in righteousness." The word "righteousness" is described for us in the Encyclopedia Britannica as "right thinking." We are also told there is a three-fold cord that is not quickly broken. It is built like the ark, on three levels: the physical level here, the psychological level, and the spiritual level. Tonight, we are taking three characters of Scripture: Esau, Jacob, and Israel. I think I have broken this cord - in fact I am convinced of it, so I would like to share with you what I know of these levels. They are not persons as we are; they are states of consciousness through which the immortal soul passes on its way to God.

We read this story in the 25th chapter of Genesis. We are told that Rebecca was childless and that she and Isaac prayed to God that they may be blessed with a child, and God responded. That is what we are told all through the Bible, this response to prayer for a child. In this case they are twins. And the Lord said unto her: "Two nations are in your womb and two people born of you shall be divided; one shall be stronger than the other and the elder shall serve the younger." Now here is a prophecy, before the children were brought into the world, which one would excel. Here is predestination - you cannot interpret it in any other way. They are brought into the world, they haven't committed either good or evil, and yet one is predestined to excel. He is the younger - Jacob, the supplanter - and the first one, Esau, must serve him. But I tell you: these are states of consciousness. Or we can take them on different levels.

We are told in the same chapter of Genesis that the first son he gave me was red all over, like a hairy animal, so they called him Esau. His other name was Edom - like Adam - spelled in the same way [in Hebrew], the red earth, the red being. That's the first one, who must now serve the younger. The second came out holding in his hand the heel of the first, and he was called Jacob, the supplanter.

We are told the first one was a hunter, a man of the fields, and the second one was a smooth-skinned lad who lived in a tent. So on this level it is the outer and the inner man. No matter how hairless you seem to be, just put a magnifying glass on the body and you will see the body is completely covered with hair (you may call it a fuzz but it is hair) and the most external thing in this world of man is hair; next will be skin. The second one has no hair, so, hairless - that is the inner man. Putting it now into our language so that you and I can understand it and apply it, the outer man is a man of sense. I am in this room right now and everything seems so real, more real than anything else in the world. I know this room by reason of my bodily organs. My senses allow it and my reason dictates it. This is fact; all this is real.

There is an inner man and he is skilled in arranging things so that they reach to desired ends, not based upon the evidence of the senses. The inner man, by standing here, could desire to be elsewhere and deny the evidence of my senses, denying reason, dare to assume I am where I would like to be, and rearrange the furniture of my mind. Instead of using this to tell me I am here, I use other furniture - objects of my mind. Here I rearrange it and remain faithful to that state until it takes on the tones of reality. And when it seems to be sensory vivid and I open my eyes upon it, I am shocked to find I am still here. That is the inner man, called Jacob, the supplanter - he takes the place of the outer man. He supplanted his brother twice. First, he took his birthright, then he took his blessing; so, these are the two in conflict and the whole story is one of conflict.

Eventually, after unnumbered ages, Jacob will be given the name of Israel, "a man after God's own heart." It seems to come soon, but it doesn't really. No one knows the length of time between the awakening of these two states of consciousness and the fulfillment in the form of Israel. But you must read the Bible from all angles.

First Esau is Edom. In the story of Job, the hero is an Edomite, all the characters are Edomites, and the whole play is laid in Edom. "Edom" means the "red earth". We are told the first one to make a name for himself by subduing all the Edomites was named David.[7] He is the first king of Israel chosen by Jehovah. Saul was chosen by the people, but

---

[7] *Read it in 2 Samuel, 8 -*

rejected by Jehovah. Here is one, David, chosen by Jehovah - the first king of Israel. Israel means "a man after my own heart. "Behold an Israelite indeed in whom there is no guile." That is what he said when he saw Nathaniel, and only the pure in heart can see God. "I have found David, a man after my own heart, one who could subdue the Edomite." That comes way beyond this initial story of the parents of the two boys. It is all in us.

I am told, as you are told tonight, that it is possible that I can assume I am the man I would like to be. If I dare to remain faithful to that assumption and not waver in it - and to the degree that I am loyal to that assumption - it will crystallize and become a fact. I need not appeal to any person in the world to help me. I can do it all by myself if I know of the existence of the Being in me who is skilled in arranging things so that it leads to a desired end. How would I arrange the furniture of the mind to reach the desired end, but name the end first - the end is where I begin. My end is my beginning.

This is a very simple story; it is a true story. A man - an engineer who had never earned twenty thousand a year, he had never earned beyond ten - I said to him: "Where would you work if you made your twenty thousand?" He said: "I have picked out the job - they don't know it, but the building is on Madison Avenue. I know exactly the floor, I have ridden up in the elevator, I have gotten off at the floor and walked into the office. I know where I would sit were it true that I work there; where I will hang my hat and when I take off my coat where I will put it. I know exactly what I will do." I said: "Al right, now stand in that elevator and go up, see it stop at the floor and get off, walk right into the place, take off your hat and jacket, and just simply be natural in the job." Within two weeks he was on that job at twenty thousand a year.

He traveled all over the near east aiding in the building of dams and all kinds of these fantastic things he loved, after this last world war. One day he didn't feel well, closed his eyes and made his exit from this world, but he had five years to exercise his Jacob. What does it matter when we go from this sphere? It doesn't really matter. Before he made his exit he discovered David, and if there is evidence of a thing, what does it matter what you or I or anyone thinks about it or wish about it? But he proved it and lived by it for five years. I can multiply that by hundreds and hundreds of the exercising of Jacob.

Jacob comes second - bear this in mind. The whole vast world, three billion of us, we only know the existence of Esau. We know the man, he was born in a certain social structure, and that's it. He had no financial, social, intellectual, or other support behind him, and life is rugged. That is Esau, that is Edom. And then comes this story and he is made aware of another one that will be brought forth, and that one's name is Jacob, the supplanter. And you tell him what you would do were you he, and he tries it, and he does it, and quite often having done it once, he forgets it and he goes back and serves Esau.

Then comes that moment in time when he hits the third level of the ark, the spiritual level, and knows the thing is literally true on the third level. All these stories are literally true on the spiritual level. It is only the psychological level [where] there is something different. Like I stand here and assume I am elsewhere and I see the world as I would if I was standing there physically, then I open my eyes to find there isn't any difference, and I am shocked I am not actually there. I have gone to prepare a place, having gone to prepare a place I returned here, but I will now move across a bridge of incidents - a little series of events, leading from where I am physically to where I am consciously. I try it again, and as I try it and it works I am becoming aware of Jacob.

What about Esau? Jacob wrestled all through the night of human darkness and ignorance with the Lord himself, but he couldn't grant him what he asked for. He had to change his name before he could give him what he asked for. He changed it from Jacob, the deceiving one; for he deceived his father-in-law, his brother, his father - he deceived everyone. But even though he deceived them, he was God's chosen vessel.

I deceive myself when I stand here and persuade myself that I am elsewhere. I deceive myself when I persuade myself you are what you would like to be. If I forget what you told me you are, and think only what you would like to be, and when I am self-persuaded you are such a person, I am self-deceived. So, Jacob is the deceiving one. He comes into the presence of his father; he has no hair, while his brother is covered all over with red hair. And with the aid of Rebecca - the mother, he takes two goats, slaughters the goats, takes the hair, the skin, covers his hands and the nape of his neck, and puts on the robe of his brother that he may deceive the father when he comes into the father's presence. The father said: "Who are you?" He said: "I am your son, Esau." He said: "Come closer, I can't see you, come closer that I may feel you." So, he comes closer and the father feels him, and he said: "You feel like Esau but your voice sounds like Jacob." He said: "I am your son Esau."

He persuaded the father he was Esau and the father gave him the blessing that belonged to Esau. Then, when the father had completely acted, he could not now take it back, because God swears by himself and cannot take back his oath or change it. When he saw Esau coming from the hunt to discover his treachery, he said: "He is well-named, for twice he has taken from me," supplanted me. So the father gave Jacob the blessing.

I clothe myself in imagery by rearranging the furniture of the mind, seeing myself and having you see me, as I would like to be seen by you. When I see you in my mind's eye seeing me as you would see me were it true that I am what I am assuming that I am, then I am pre-clothed. Now to what degree can I fool myself? To what degree can I actually become all the characters and play now the part of Isaac and let myself be Isaac and believe what I am doing is real and true? Can I believe in the reality of that imaginal act? Yes, I've done it unnumbered times and it worked. Whenever I do it with persuasion to the point of acceptance, it worked, and I found my Jacob.

Now, there is another one. I have to find Israel. Israel is on the highest level, a man after God's own heart. How do you find him? There is not a thing in this world you can do to find him; it is revealed. It just happens, and this is how it happened to me. One night I saw these two fantastic creatures; I saw Esau and he is just as he is described, covered from the crown of his head to the sole of his feet with red hair, just like a huge big ape. And here, Jacob - instead of being a man, Jacob is the most glorious female you could ever imagine. Here is an angel beyond angels, and here is Esau, this monster-thing thriving on violence, thriving on everything that is evil in this world, living on it.

And I thought when I saw the two of them that they existed independent of my perception of them. I didn't know they did not. I did not know I had never severed the umbilical cord, that they are my children. I am the being spoken of as Rebecca, who gave birth to both of them, one, the embodiment of any unlovely thought I have ever entertained. Every time I have ever exercised my imagination unlovingly on behalf of another, it simply energized this unlovely creature. Every time I acted or reacted violently, I fed and energized Esau. And looking at Esau, I had a desire without turning to anyone to ask their help or to pledge myself in their presence, and I pledged myself that I would redeem this monster if it took me to eternity. Such a creature should not live in this world and I, in my ignorance, gave him birth - this monstrous thing that fed and lived on violence. In my blindness he would whisper in my ear throughout the 24-hour day, yes, even in my dreams and urge me to violence and urge me to react in the unlovely way.

Then I saw what he was. I still did not know at that moment that he was not independent of my perception of him. But I said I would redeem him. At that very moment that I said I would redeem him if it took me eternity, I discovered he was not an entity as you are; he was nothing more than an embodied force. Here was all my misused, misspent energy throughout eternity, for this monstrous thing before my eyes melted and left no trace of ever having been present; but as it melted, all the energy that it embodied came to me, it returned to me who gave it.

I have never felt such power in my life. Everything came back to me and this glorious creature that was the personification of all my noble acts, my lovely acts, my ever-loving thought, every state - she glowed, and this one melts before my eyes. So, I tell you: you will meet both of them. They are present now. You can't see them at the moment but they are present wherever you go, but I tell you of them after you exercise Jacob. Every time you persuade yourself of something loving, something lovely - even though reason at the moment denies it and your senses deny it, everything denies it - to that degree you are so persuaded, you are feeding this glorious creature and you are denying food to this monster. It isn't his fault; we gave him birth. As the poet said: "Alas, two souls are housed within thy breast, one to heaven does aspire; the other to earth doth cling." Two are housed in the breast of every being and that is part of the structure of this world. Everyone is bringing into the world these two and they are invisible until that moment in time when you wrestle the testing of God and your name is changed from Jacob, to Israel. Then you will know why David, the true king of Israel, was the first to make a name for himself by being the first to subdue the Edomites.

You will see the Edomite embodied in a single lad, and that being is a monster; his name is Esau. You will redeem him not by blows, as the historians tell you, for they tell you that he [i.e. David] slaughtered in one night 18,000 Edomites. No, he didn't slaughter any 18,000 Edomites as individual units. He conquered the whole of Edom, while knowing the embodiment of all was Esau. And when he melted the whole of Esau, he was a man after God's own heart. So, we are told: "I have found in David a man after my own heart, and he is mine forever, he is my son, I will go before him - I will be his father and he will be my son."[8] And that one is being brought forth from the body; it is God's only begotten, who becomes, in time, the father of that from which it emerged, in Christ Jesus. You are giving birth to Christ Jesus, that is, the father of David. And David will call him: "My father, my Lord, and the rock of my salvation."[9] Every being in the world because of this conflict within himself is practically molding and shaping within himself Christ Jesus.

Paul tells us:[10] "My little children, with whom I am again in travail until Christ be formed in you!" And when Christ is born in you, it is because he comes from a heart which is the heart of God; and so, "I have found in David a man after my own heart." The whole vast world on the outside - that is Edom, that is Esau, and the victory belongs to Jacob. It is prophesied: "There are two nations within your womb, and two people born of you shall be divided - one shall be stronger than the other and the elder shall serve the younger." This is the elder that comes first, so reason tells you it can't be and your senses confirm what reason dictates. But the prophecy is the victory belongs to the younger, it belongs to Jacob, and Jacob is your ability, your skill in rearranging things so as to determine or predetermine an outcome. How would I feel tonight were I . . . and you name it. What would I see were it true, then see it; and how would I feel were it true, well then, feel it. What would I say to my friends were it true, then say it, not audibly for this means in the psychological meaning. You say it inwardly, so you talk to yourself inwardly as though you spoke outwardly. You carry on these mental conversations from premise of fulfilled desire, you talk to all you friends on these premises - and that is Jacob. But do it lovingly. The more you do it lovingly the nearer you are to meeting God in that successful resting message.

---

[8] *Acts 13:24*
[9] *Psalm 89*
[10] *Gal. 4:19*

And so, one day it's going to happen. When it happens you will say exactly what he said.[11] "I have seen God face to face and yet my life is preserved." Here I stood in the presence of God and I didn't know it. This is the house of the Lord and I didn't know it. So he takes the stone on which he slept that night to mark the place of the house of God and he calls it Bethel, the house of the Lord, the house of God. And in this dream who did he see? He saw the contact between infinity and finite man, for here a ladder rested on earth and stretched to the heavens and above it all stood God; and he saw on that ladder, ascending and descending, God. The Bible translates the word Elohim -"angel". It is not angel, it is Elohim. It was God rising and descending, and above it all stood the Lord. The Lord said to him: "I am the Lord, the God of Abraham your father, and the God of Isaac." If you read it as an historical document, Abraham was not his father, Isaac was his father. If you read it through the eyes of the spirit the voice is telling the truth: Abraham is the father of all above you. We all come out of Abraham. So, here I am the father - I, the Lord and God of Abraham, your father.

Now we go to the first verse of the book of Matthew, which is the book of genealogy of Jesus Christ, son of David, son of Abraham, all coming out of Abraham. All the prophecies are made to him. Then comes the most complex thing of the battle within man. No special event, because he is the Edomite of Edomites; his name is Job. The conflict within him, and Jehovah spoke to him and said: "Why should a mere man sin?" and he asks three very important questions: "Do you know the period of gestation of the wild goat? Do you know the habits of the wild ass? Can you domesticate the wild ox?" You read that and you wonder what it is all about, and what beautiful imagery.

In my vision I saw Christ as the ox, as the wild ass, as the wild goat. Was not the wild goat the substitute for Isaac the sacrifice of the sin of the world? And he found the wild goat. Can you tell me the period of gestation of the wild goat? How long will it take Christ in man to really come to earth? Can you domesticate the wild ox? How long does it take you to take that wonderful imagination of yours and actually tame it? Everything denies it, so you go wild in your reactions and you still remain the wild ox. Can you domesticate the wild goat? Do you know the habits

---

[11] *Genesis*

of the wild ass? Are we not told, a stupid man will get understanding when the wild ass's colt is for a man? And did he not ride the ass in the most triumphant ride in the world into Jerusalem? He came riding on an ass. He couldn't if it was still wild, it had to be controlled, it had to be domesticated, broken in. So he comes riding on that which he had tamed, his own wonderful human Imagination.

Take that Imagination of yours - which is God in man - and no matter what the appearance seems to be, what would you like it to be? Well then, see it as though it were. Believe me, imagining creates reality. All things are created by him. I tell you I have proved to my own satisfaction that imagining creates reality. Therefore, if I know it and live by it, I have found him, and I too can ride triumphantly on this domesticated wild, wild beast. You want to ride it, but normally, for the wild ass was given first to man; and so Christ in man was wild, but man didn't know it and he starts with the state of consciousness called Jacob. I have told you the story - I hope you believed it. Every time you try it, even if you fail, Jacob is being exercised. But, may I tell you: obviously you cannot fail, because it is predestined.

Jacob cannot fail. A cue is given to us as to who he is when we see the one of the twelve sons he loved most. He loved Joseph most of all, for Joseph was the comfort of his old age. Joseph was born of the woman he wanted most, but in his conflict he had to marry Leah. Then, after he had served another seven years - seven for Leah - he was tricked. As he had tricked the father-in-law, the father-in-law tricked him. Then he had to serve another seven years, this time to get Rachael; and out of Rachel comes Joseph and his last, Benjamin. But Joseph was his love, the joy of his old age, and Joseph was a dreamer. Listen to the words: "Behold this dreamer cometh, let us sell him, let us kill him." He could not only dream, he could interpret dreams, for this faculty in man that dreams is man's imagination, and any interpreter of dreams is man's imagination. "Behold the dreamer cometh, let us kill him." Judah says: "No", let us sell him to the Ishmaelites as the caravan moves on toward Egypt." So they sold him, the dreamer. That is what everyone does in this world. But the dreamer rose to the heights of wealth and saved them in their famine. So, the dreamer in man will save him - that's Joseph. But what a long trail in time between the moment when they sold the dreamer into slavery to the one called David - who brings out the darkness, who brings out the Edomite, and makes for himself a name of names in all of Israel. So God said of him: "I have found a man after my own heart."

The day will come when you will prove every word I have told you tonight. You will meet these souls just as I have described them. You will meet the most radiant Being, and you know who she is. It doesn't make sense, but these two are not detached from you. They are all in you, and at that moment in time, they seem to be external to you, but the umbilical cord has not been severed. You will see the only embodied enemies. Instead of spending any time to correct that mistake, right before your very eyes it melted, but it doesn't vanish. All the enemies are there to be changed by you. And you know the words: "Nothing is lost in all my holy mountain." In all my wanderings I thought it was lost, and yet nothing is lost - it was embodied in a monstrous thing. But then it came back; all that I had accused as enemy wasn't gone or lost, it returned.

It caused me frightful suffering in the interval that it first began to form within me, and I gave my whole body and my life over to my senses, to passion based upon this garment that was hairy from head to feet. Then I began to work on something entirely different, a Jacob that was smooth of skin that no one can see. He was the supplanter. I heard about him, I began to seek him and it worked; and then one day I saw that he was not forever an invisible state. He became a concrete reality. I saw him, and what beauty! And I saw Esau, but redeemed Esau. Jacob does not need redeeming. It will not fail you, but these are the three states through which the immortal soul must pass. You are doing it now anyway.

Everything you said within yourself is being fulfilled. If you say: "I don't believe it," it's perfectly all right, that's your privilege, but that is father to anything you did to these two. They are struggling now within your womb. For long before they come out and you see them the struggle is on, because she asked the question: "Why is this so, why do I live if this fight is so within me?" Then the answer: he tells us: "There are two nations" and the war is on, and one will serve the other. He tells exactly which will do which - the elder will serve the younger. The one that comes first - Esau, the elder - and he serves the younger.

Who is he? What is Jacob's name? The supplanter. He looks at the world and he doesn't like it. Like that vision I had on Fifth Avenue.

Looking at an empty lot I would say: "I remember when it was an empty lot." It still is an empty lot to my outer senses, but I am not interested in my outer senses. I would build a word picture as I desired this lot to be. I would say: "I remember when it was an empty lot," and still to outer appearances it is an empty lot, but not to me or to those who had that so-called dream.[12] That is exercising the inner man, exercising Jacob.

The day will come when God, and only God, knows. He sees the heart just as he wants it and you are wrestling all alone with yourself. Then one day, he sees the heart, and the heart is owned by one called David, "A man after my own heart." Suddenly he sees David, and David is his only begotten son. David reveals to him who he is: God the father. Everyone will one day find David, a man after God's own heart and then he will reveal to you the one you have been seeking through all eternity! You are God the Father.

Now let us go into the silence.

## Question Period:

**Q.** What does it mean: "I beheld Satan falling like lightning from Heaven?

**A.** That is when the disciples returned, glorifying God and telling what marvelous things they had seen with the teachings to all kinds of people, casting out the unlovely things in people. Then he rejoiced when he heard of the great works being done by those whom he had taught and he said: "I beheld Heaven." Well, Satan is really the state. Satan is only the embodiment of unbelief. He saw the entire thing fall, because here they could have done nothing unless they believed. "According to your belief be it done unto you. Your faith has made you whole." So when the seventy returned filled with good news of what they had done through the teaching, he saw unbelief tumble from Heaven, for Heaven is within you. Therefore, it is always the state within you that dictates policy - what you will believe, what you will not believe. Then, in that Heavenly state, unbelief is cast out.

---

[12] *June 15, 1962*

# Eschatology
# The Doctrine *of the* End

Eschatology is the doctrine of the last days. It is the dramatic end of human history and the beginning of eternal salvation. When you, an individual arrive at that point in time, human history and the appearance of the Son or man (who is God) come together. This will happen in you after the tribulation of human experience, and of that day and hour only the Father in you knows.

Although God the Father appears to be another, He is your very Self, as His spirit is in you. Were this not so, you could not commune with Him or He with you. He tells us to: "Bring my sons from afar and my daughters from the end of the earth. Bring them all who are called by my name, whom I created for my glory, whom I formed and made." You were created for God's glory, His glory will not be given to another, therefore you must be the one who created you. This you will know when you experience eschatology. It comes at the end of human tribulation, when all of the parts have been played, therefore envy no one, the part they are paying, for you have either played it already or you will play it, for you cannot come to this dramatic end until you have played all of the parts, and of that day only the Father within you knows.

Eschatology was predicted and was fulfilled in vision. Always bear in mind that all of the stories recorded in scripture are visions. The Book of Isaiah begins: "This is the vision of Isaiah, the son of Amos." He tells you it is a vision and the sixty-six chapters do not deny it, modify it, or in any way contradict his words. We speak of the visions of Obadiah, the visions of Ezekiel, and are told that: "The word of the Lord came to Jeremiah." These are all visions, not secular history at all.

In the 42nd chapter of Isaiah, we read: "Behold, the former things have come to pass and new I now declare; before they spring forth I tell you of them." A literal rendering of the first part of that verse could be: "The former things, behold they have come, but man will not believe the individual who experienced them."

Jesus Christ is not a man. He has revealed himself in me and will reveal himself in all even though the world is looking for something entirely different. The visions of the prophets will unfold in individual man when he enters the state called Paul. And when you enter that state, your mystical experiences will reveal the end of your tribulation of human experience and your entry into the kingdom of God.

The entire eschatology of the Old Testament is the coming of Jehovah. He came, but - expecting a physical person to come from without, they would not believe him.

But Jehovah comes only to fulfill what He had predicted through his prophets, saying: "Behold the former things have come and are here now." The former predictions of the prophets become your experiences of the one who fulfills scripture, for man fulfills the prophecy of himself in the last days.

God, prophesying what he would do through his prophets, entered into the limitation of and took upon himself the restriction of man. The power and wisdom to create emptied himself of all that was his and, taking upon himself the form of a slave, was born in the likeness of man. Spirit became obedient unto death, even death upon the cross of man. And when an individual man told the story of how the prophecies unfolded in him, no one would believe his story.

So today we still have that fundamental rock called Israel. Their calendar year is now approaching 6,000, because to them He has not come. It is only when eschatology comes to the individual does his BC turn into A.D. The Jew will date their letters as the year 1969 because it is part of the world of Caesar, but believing Jehovah has not yet come, in his faith, the Jew keeps alive the long passage of time. But Jehovah comes in an entirely different way. He inspired the prophets to record the visions the individual will experience, personally.

Now if God - being Spirit - is known in a vision, what must you do to experience Him? You must reenact the drama within yourself! The resurrection takes place within. The birth foretold to Abraham takes place within. The three who bear witness to the birth are not seen approaching, but suddenly appear within. And the story of the serpent in the wilderness is fulfilled within when you become the serpent and ascend into heaven as the Lord God Jehovah.

Who would have thought - I know I didn't - that the story recorded in the 22nd and 53rd chapters of Isaiah would be experienced in one night? Remember: when the prophets recorded their visions they were written out, but not paragraphed or made into chapter form. In fact, they were not even punctuated and often one word flowed into the other. It is man who has taken the manuscript and given it punctuation, verses, paragraphs, and chapters.

In the 53rd chapter of Isaiah, the question is asked: "Who has believed our report and to whom has the arm of the Lord been revealed?" One night in vision I found myself in a room much like this one. I was seated on the floor facing twelve men, explaining the word of God when one quickly rose quickly and departed. As he left, I intuitively knew he was going to tell the authorities what he had heard. Then a tall, handsome man about 6'4" tall, dressed in costly robes, entered. Because of his importance we all rose and stood at attention as he walked straight as an arrow to the end of the room, turned right, walked to the end, turned right again and came down the center to confront me. Taking a mallet and a wooden peg, he hammered the peg into my right shoulder. I felt every blow, yet it was not painful. Then he took a sharp instrument and with one quick, circular motion he severed my sleeve, tore it off and discarding it, he stretched out his arms forming the cross, embraced me, and kissed me on the right side of my neck as I - in turn - kissed him on the right side of his neck. And as the vision faded I saw the severed sleeve. It was a lovely shade of baby blue. His robe was costly, but mine was the priceless robe of light, light blue.

So now I know whom I have believed, for that night the arm of the Lord was revealed in me, and the 53rd chapter of Isaiah was fulfilled as well as the 22nd chapter of Isaiah. In this chapter we are told that he puts a peg into the shoulder of the one he has chosen, and on that peg all of the burdens of Israel are hung until the peg is broken. Then the utensils of the temple fall, for he has played his part.

Eschatology will never be understood as long as you look for someone on the outside to fulfill it. It an only be understood when you, personally experience it. Then you will tell your experiences to those who will listen, and some will believe you while others will disbelieve.

Eschatology is not the end of the world, as people believe. This past year a crowd left California and moved to Georgia and parts east, believing an earthquake would suddenly appear which would completely inundate us, and for the first time in recorded history, the east experienced an earthquake which shook twelve states.

What does it matter if an earthquake comes when there is no death? The individual who seems to die, in truth is restored to life in a 20-year old body to continue life in the environment best suited for the work still to be done in him. Cast in a role he has not yet played, he will continue life as we know it here, until he has played all of the tribulations of human experience. Then and only then will he arrive at eschatology - the day of the Lord - and only the Father knows when that day will appear.

I don't care who you are - you are destined to experience eschatology, for it was God's purpose to give himself to you and God is able to fulfill his purpose. He created you to radiate his glory and be the express image of his person.

You cannot stop God from fulfilling his purpose, but you will not arrive at that moment called eschatology until you have played all the parts - be they good, bad, or indifferent. So I say, envy no one. It doesn't matter what they have done, are doing, or will do; do not envy or pity anyone, for you have either already played that part, or you will.

The Bible records every conceivable evil in the world that man could do to man and describes it openly. And you have played, or will play, every part before the last days come upon you, and in that day, events of scripture will unfold in you in a dramatic form imaginable. You will be possessed and find yourself the center of the entire Bible. As scripture reveals itself in you, you will discover from experience that you are the Lord Jesus Christ. And when you share your experience with others, they will question how a little nonentity who suffers and has nothing the world he would brag about could dare to make this bold assumption. They will think of you as blaspheming God, just as they accused him, claiming he blasphemed by stating, I and my Father are one, that when you see me you have seen the Father; that if you really knew me, you would know my Father also, but you know neither me nor my Father, for my Father is playing the part that I am.

And then one night in vision, I fulfilled the 42nd Psalm. That night, in vision I found myself leading an enormous crowd in gay procession to the house of God as a voice rang out: "And God walks with them." A woman at my side asked the voice: "If God walks with us, where is he?"

and the voice replied: "At your side." Turning to her left she looked into my face and, laughing hysterically said, "What, Neville is God?" and the voice replied, "Yes, in the act of waking." Then the voice spoke in the depths of my soul, saying: "I laid myself down within you to sleep and as I slept I dreamed a dream. I dreamed..." and, knowing exactly what he was going to say, I became so excited I actually nailed myself upon this body in the same manner tradition tells us he was nailed upon the cross, but it was not a painful experience. Six vortices, each an ecstatic, joyful feeling, hold me here.

Now I know that no man took (or takes) my life, for I lay it down myself. I know I have the power to lay it down and the power to take it up again; for I, God the Father, deliberately took upon myself this limitation upon myself. When I heard the voice that night say: "I laid myself down within you to sleep, and as I slept I dreamed a dream," I knew he was telling me that he was I and when the dream is over and he awakes I would be He, radiating His glory and bearing the express image of His person.

This is not for me alone, but for all. Listen to the words: "The glory that thou gavest me I would give to them that they may be one even as we are one." I have told you of the glory that is now mine, thereby giving you the glory that we may be one. I in you and thou in me, that we may be made perfectly one. I have made God's name known to you and I will make it known that the love by which I am loved may be in you. Not less love, but the same love, so that the whole may become one love!

In the end everyone will experience the whole Bible and tell it as I am telling it now. A few will believe but the majority will not. That's all right, for all of the tribulations of human experience must be fulfilled, with no omissions. Today you may be one of the so-called beautiful people, possessing inherited wealth. You may be one of the ten best dressed women and spend a quarter of a million dollars on clothes to create the part you are playing. But tomorrow, even if you haven't played it, you may play the part of a scrub woman, for every part must be played before you can arrive at eschatology.

Having played every part as recorded in scripture, when I saw a man betray me I knew I had played the part of the betrayer, for I have fulfilled scripture.

Everyone must play it all, if not on this stage, then on another, for when you leave this set on the stage of life, although you are no longer seen by the audience here, you are not dead, but have entered another stage in the great theater called life, to continue the work that is still to be done in you, until all of the parts in the play have been played.

Eschatology is not the end of the earth, but the end of human history and the beginning of eternal salvation. It is the abrupt cleavage between this world and the transcendental world of God. It is your entrance into an entirely different world where you radiate God's glory which you create by your very being, for you are now the Father. God the Father created you to radiate his glory and bear the express image of His person in that world. I cannot describe it because there are no images on earth to aid me. Life there is entirely different from this one, for there you are not some little pygmy, but God Himself, completely equipped to do it all!

So, if you condemn someone, the chances are you have not played the part he is playing, but will play it tomorrow, for condemnation simply moves you closer to the fulfillment of what you have condemned. Let no one judge you and don't judge another, for you know too much now. It is my hope you have played all the parts and that tonight your eschatology will come. Sacred history has been brought to its climax, and fulfilled in Jesus Christ, but Jesus Christ in you is the one who does it.

Addressing God as, "O righteous Father", John said: "I in them and thou in me." Now, if God the Father is in me, and I am in you, is He not in you also? Yes, God the Father is in you and Christ, his God's creative power, is in you as the pattern man who must fulfill scripture. The plan was made for, and erupts in Christ - the Christ in you. He is your hope of glory, for you are the one spoken of as Abraham.

In the state called Abraham the promise was made that you would have a child. So what part are you playing then the child appears? Abraham looked up to see three men standing before him. He thought they were messengers of the Lord for he did not realize he was the Lord himself. It is said he did not see them approaching they came so suddenly. And when the prophecy is fulfilled your attention is diverted for a few seconds by an unearthly wind, and when you look back those that you did not see approaching are sitting where your body was, for your body is now gone. The body has been removed because you only wore it for a little while, but while you wore it something happened in you.

Now a lady wrote this past week, saying: "In my dream I was shoveling dirt. Although it seemed as though I was digging in the earth, I knew I was digging in my own brain." That's a lovely vision and a true one. Everything takes place in the brain - the earth, for man is made up of the dust of the earth, so her vision was perfect. She was digging in her own brain. For she is on the verge, although I cannot tell her the day or the hour, for only the Father in her knows.

If you will read the Book of John - which differs somewhat from the synoptics, you will discover that John pinpoints the day the vision will occur, stating that the birth, followed by the resurrection, will take place between 6:00 P.M. on Sunday and 6:00 P.M. on Monday. That is when it happened in me. I went to bed on Sunday evening about 11:00 P.M. and awoke, was born from above, and resurrected at 4:00 A.M. on Monday morning. You will follow the same pattern. Having entered the world before the coming of Jehovah, you entered the world from B.C. and when it happens your world turns into the year of the Lord, A.D.

The Old Testament is crowded with eschatology - the coming of Jehovah. He came but was not recognized because it was not what people expected. But He is coming in your world and you are going to fulfill scripture. When you realize you are the central character of the Bible, you are going to feel so wonderful. I cannot tell you the thrill that is in store for you when you experience everything written there. Even though it has happened to others, scripture is all about you, because in the end there is no other. In that day, you will know that I dwell in them and thou in me, and we, all gathered together are perfect in that one body, one Spirit, one Lord, one God and Father of all.

You will not have a different son from the speaker. We have the same son. When I tell this to priests, rabbis and ministers, they throw up their hands in holy horror and claim I have taken all of their religion from them. What they have been taught is true on a certain level of awareness, but I am speaking from experience. I have experienced scripture. I know it is true, but it is not what the world teaches.

Jesus Christ is God the Father and Jesus Christ is in you. One day you will find out that you are God the father and because you are you will produce a son to bear witness to that fact. Now no one knows who God the Father is, except his son who comes into your world to reveal you to yourself. And when he appears you don't have to ask him who he is; the minute you see him you know exactly who he is and he knows who you are. There is no uncertainty as to this relationship. To know that you are God the Father, yet while you remain here in the world of Caesar you will continue to wear the little garment that suffers, as all garments do. But after you have experienced eschatology and leave this little garment behind, you will no longer be restored to life, for you will have come to the end of human history.

In the Book of Acts it is said that Paul remained at home, talking from morning to night about the word of God and the kingdom of heaven. It does not say how Paul departed, in spite of tradition where they claim he was a martyr. Paul was not murdered. The word "martyr" means "witness". He was a witness, yes, a witness to the truth of God's word, for the word is true, and someone had to witness it.

So when it happens to you, you will tell it. You may not speak from the platform, as I do, but you will tell it. You can't restrain the impulse as we are told in Jeremiah: "If I say I will not mention him or speak any more in his name, there is in my heart, as it were, a burning fire and I am tired of holding it in and I cannot." It's simply something within you and you cannot stop telling your story. You will be compelled to make known unto them God's name and the love by which you are loved, that that same love may be in them.

Now, Jesus Christ does not stand before himself and call himself Father. God's only begotten son, David, stands before Jesus Christ in you, and calls you father as he called me Father. Then you will know we are the same Jesus Christ.

I can say to every one of you: you are going to have this experience and know from experience who you really are. There are not a lot of Jesus Christ's running around, there is only God the Father. If I am the father of God's only begotten Son as told me in the 2nd Psalm and you have the same experience, then you and I are the same Father. And if the whole world has the same experience - and they will - then we are the one God and Father of all, are we not? So John's prayer is that all will become one as he has become one Father. And he speaks of the glory recorded in Isaiah, saying: "The glory thou gavest me, I have given them." God didn't keep a little glory for himself and share the rest. It's the same glory, because there cannot be another. So in the end there is only one God, only one Lord, only one Father, and only one Son and you will be the Father of that son, as I know I am the Father of that one and only son.

This is eschatology - the arrival of the end of the tribulation of human experience and the beginning of eternal salvation. And, although you may not remember, you had to have played every part in this world to arrive at the fulfillment of scripture. The blind man, the deaf man, the poor man, the rich man, the beggar, the thief, the murderer, the betrayer, the betrayed - you name it and scripture has mentioned it. You can't name one vile or evil state that is not described openly in scripture. And you have played them all, or you will.

I think you who come here have played them all or you would not be this constant. You would find something far more interesting tonight, raining as it is, than to be here. So, in the not distant future you will be fulfilling scripture and experiencing the thrill of the events s they happen. Today we watched the inauguration of a new president. It was a marvelous production, but it pales into insignificance compared to the dramatic quality that possesses you when scripture unfolds within you.

Can you imagine waking and coming out of your skull as one coming out of a womb? Then five months later finding your son who calls you Father? These two different events are recorded in the 9th chapter of Isaiah as: "To us a child is born; to us a son is given." The child appears to bear witness to your birth, and the son is given to witness your Fatherhood. You may think the child and the son are the same, but they are not. They signify two dramatic events within you. I am sure our new president felt thrilled to be sworn in by our chief justice, but the thrill you will experience when scripture unfolds within you is far greater, for these experiences belong to the transcendental world of God, and not to this mortal world of history.

Can you imagine the thrill that possesses you when, like a fiery serpent, you ascend into heaven and it reverberates like thunder? Having played that part of one in generation, you are regenerated and all that you have ever done is forgiven.

I have shared my visions of the last days with you. They will come, but only after you have experienced all the trials and tribulations of human experience. Don't try to remember them for God, in his infinite mercy has hidden the memory from you for a purpose and in the end it is all washed away anyway. "Though your sins are as scarlet they shall be as white as snow," so it really doesn't matter. But I urge you to condemn no one, for you have played the part he (or she) is now playing or you will play it.

It's a horrible play, but in the end when eschatology unfolds within you, you will understand the meaning behind it all.

Now let us go into the silence.

# Eschatology
## The Drama *of the* End

The word "disciple" means "learner", and anyone who hears God's pattern of salvation from one who has experienced it and believes, hungering to learn more, is a disciple. Tradition tells us Peter, James, and John were disciples. No, you are a disciple if you believe my words!

Now, when I speak of Jesus, I am speaking of the pattern man, for "He has made known unto me the purpose of his will which he set forth in Christ as a plan, a pattern for the fullness of time." That pattern has unfolded in me and I can tell you from experience: Jesus Christ is the unfoldment of the Father and the Son. If you believe me, you are my disciples.

Now, I have a few perfectly marvelous eschatological dreams to share with you. Here is an experience of one who heard and believes. This is his dream: He said: "You were on the platform, teaching. Although you smiled at me there was great intensity in your eyes. Taking a golden arrow from your side, you placed it in your bow and shot it directly at me. As it came toward me I could read the word, "resurrection" imprinted upon it as it penetrated my forehead. Then you shot a second arrow, which read "David" and it penetrated my chest. The third arrow carried the word "ascension" and it penetrated my belly, touching my spine. The fourth arrow carried no word, only a white dove, and as it hit me I felt as though every pore of my body had been struck. I have never known such ecstasy of love before. I felt like a spiritual fountain of pure, pure love."

"The following night in a dream, a man I have never seen approached me. Radiating love he said: 'I am preparing a great feast and I will come on the seventeenth to take you with me.'"

Now this could literally mean the seventeenth, but in symbolism seventeen is a marvelous number. In Hebrew you do not write the number seventeen as "one-seven," but "seven-ten," denoting greater importance. This number first appears in the 37th chapter of Genesis as

"Joseph was seventeen years old." Then in the 47th chapter of Genesis, Joseph and his father are taught by Jacob for seventeen years. So seventeen, denoting a combination of seven and ten, is broken down to read: seven - as spiritual perfection, and ten - as order perfection. In this gentleman's preceding vision the order was perfect, beginning with resurrection, then David, the ascension, and finally the dove who smothered him with love. Here is order perfection and spiritual perfection! I can say to him tonight: the arrows have penetrated you and nothing can stop them from reaching their destiny in the world beyond the world of dreams. You are a complete being now, as the pattern is buried in you; and in the not-distant future Jesus Christ, the pattern man, will unfold from within.

Now, the earliest gospel begins with these words: "The beginning of the gospel of Jesus Christ." The world "gospel" means "good news", not "good advice." So the gospel is "The beginning of the good news of Jesus Christ," the good news of how God actually becomes Man that Man may become God. That's the good news I share with all.

Here is another dream: This lady found herself walking with members of the group who attend these lectures. Coming towards them were groups of people moving as though being conveyed by a power not their own. The first group was dressed in black with shawls covering their heads. They seemed to be a mournful group with many of them crying. They appeared to be Catholic to her. The next group wore stern, uncompromising faces. Representing religious fundamentalists, they were self-righteous and without compassion. They were followed by a friendly group of men and women, animated, smiling, and asking questions, as seekers often do. When questioned by this group, the lady said: "You will find who you really are and who God really is, and when you do you will know it is all here." And with that remark she extended her right index finger and pointed to her forehead. Then she ran to join the group as she awoke.

In the earliest gospel you will discover that the turning point is repentance. The very first words spoken by the pattern man are: "The time is fulfilled and the kingdom of God is at hand. Repent and believe in the gospel." Believe the good news that you have heard from me. To repent is to radically change your mind. Regardless of what you believe, when God's pattern of salvation is presented, can you accept it? Can you completely turn from the belief in a physical Christ on the outside, to the belief in a man of spirit on the inside? Or are you like the foolish Galatians, before whose eyes Jesus Christ was publicly portrayed as crucified? Do you know what the word "portray" means? "To make a picture of; to describe in words; to play a part like a drama on the stage." Jesus Christ was portrayed as crucified; so "Let me ask you only this, did you receive the Spirit by the works of the law, or by hearing with faith? Are you so foolish having received the Spirit, are you now ending with the flesh?"

Repentance is turning around from the belief of a fleshly being called Jesus Christ, to the spirit that is Christ, the pattern man who is trying to awaken in you. Turn around by exercising your right to change your mind. Dare to believe the opposite, in spite of the facts that seem to be screaming at you. This is what I call "revision" and the Bible calls "repentance". To revise is to repeal and if you have repealed a thing you have changed it. You can modify your concept of Christ and not completely change it by holding onto a little bit of the physical nature; but eventually you will drop it and turn around to start moving upward with the spiritual Christ, as the pattern which must unfold in all, unfolds in you.

Now here is another dream. This lady writes: "In my dream I am at a neighbor's house which is filled with numerous people. Suddenly realizing it is my responsibility to feed them all, as I extend my hands everyone is fed. Feeling detached and no longer a part of the group, I depart to discover a shovel, a pitchfork, and a rake have been placed in front of my house. Entering the house, I find a friend there whose husband has been dead for many years. Smiling at me, she says: 'My husband wants to see you.' Going to the window and looking out I watch my friend's husband, wearing a uniform of either a general or a colonel, bring the most beautiful white horse I have ever seen into my house."[13]

As her dream continued, someone gave her a very friendly white dog, which weighed exactly sixty pounds. Taking an oval basket about 14" long, she made a little bed and placed the dog in it on its back. Then she covered it with a blanket, and as she tucked the blanket around him, he

---

[13] *The only one who rides a white horse in scripture is the Word of God called Jesus Christ. The white horse is hers, for she has the implements used to care for one: a shovel, a pitchfork and a rake -*

felt just like a baby.[14] Faithful to the pattern man, she felt the child that is promised and it didn't seem strange at all. Awakening to discover it was 6:00 o'clock in the morning, she said to herself: "I must remember the dream in detail," then she fell asleep again.

Suddenly a man is standing before her. Bending forward he removed the top of his head and said: "Look into my skull." As she looked, instead of seeing brains she saw a tiny head the size of a pin. It was perfectly formed and wearing a crown, and as she looked it seemed to grow. Then the man stood up and said: "Feel my head" and when she did, it was soft like a pillow. She then began to tell him how imagining creates reality, when he spoke, saying: "If a surgeon does not come immediately, my head will split open and I will imagine myself out of this world." Here is a perfect vision which is all scripture: The white horse – that's revelation - the whole unfolding from within – and the child in the skull.

Another lady writes, saying: "I was looking at a deep cavern in the earth watching water running into it as though from a long trough. A child, about eight months old, was sitting on its bank looking at his extended hands. You, Neville were standing high above us, looking down at the child and me. Then I heard the words: 'Can a man bear a child?' and I awoke repeating that question over and over again." Those are the very words you will find in the 30th chapter of Jeremiah, and when you begin to express scripture you are at the very end of your journey.

All of the dreams I have shared with you tonight are eschatological. Here is another one. This lady finds herself in a huge corral with an awareness of being the center of unlimited expanse. The corral gate is open, and hanging on the top of the gatepost is half of the carcass of a human being. It seemed natural for it to be there and as she looked the feeling of infinite freedom possessed her.

In the 26th chapter of the Book of Exodus, the 12th verse refers to the half curtain. The significance of the curtain is given in the 10th chapter of Hebrews, the 20th verse: "He opened a new and living way through the curtain that is his flesh." The flesh she saw represented the curtain of the temple, which is torn from top to bottom in order to free

---

[14] *A dog is the symbol of faith. Called "Caleb" in scripture, he is the only one who crosses over Jordan into the Promised Land with Joshua, the Hebraic name of Jesus -*

yourself from the world of sin and death and enter the new and living way of life. And with this experience, freedom is yours.

Now another lady wrote saying she dozed off for just a few moments to find herself in a small boat in a turbulent sea. There was no steering gear and no sails, just the mast and a crossbar like a cross on a crown. She was in the nude, and climbing the mast she extended her arms on the crossbar to use her body as the sail, that which would give power and direction towards a haven.

This experience has tremendous significance. Let me quote the 7th chapter, the 2nd verse of Daniel: "I saw in my vision by night, and behold the four winds of heaven were stirring up the deep sea." The Hebrew word translated "stirring up" is translated "labor" in the 4th chapter, the 10th verse of Micah as "like a woman in labor." So I say to her: my dear you are in labor. You sat in your chair and nodded for seemingly only a moment, but in that short interval of time you saw the depth of your own being, who is you, now in labor bringing forth God's power and wisdom, called Christ.

I can't tell you my thrill when I receive all of these letters. Every one of them is eschatology, denoting the end of the drama. That's all that matters, for the purpose of life is to fulfill scripture.

Tonight, our whole country is disturbed because of the death of a man by a man; yet I tell you: the man who was killed and the man who killed him are one, and both will be gathered together in the bosom of the Risen Lord as intimate brothers. Having played their parts in this world, they will know themselves to be brothers, with a love transcending anything known to man on earth. They did not know it, nor does the world know it, but one being played both parts and that being is God. And maybe this death – unless violence erupts and takes away its significance – will foster and further what he stood for far quicker than anything else. If on the other hand there is a denial of the sacrifice, it will again be delayed. But he of one race who was killed and he of another race who killed him are both one, for in Christ there is no bond, no free, no Greek, no Jew, no male, no female, no black, no white, no yellow, no pink, no red, just one...all are one!

So, what I am trying to say is that the culmination of the teaching of Jesus Christ is found in the thought of a mystical union of the one who hears and believes, with the Father and the Son. This is brought about through the Spirit. When you receive the Spirit by hearing with faith, you will no longer see a physical savior on the outside, for you – the son – will have found your Father – your savior – to be your very self.

I pray this night as John did in his glorious 17th chapter, saying: "O righteous Father, the world has not known thee, but I have known thee, and these believe that thou hast sent me. I have made known unto them thy name, I will make it known that the love with which thou hast loved me may be in them and I in them." Where can I go if I am going to the Father and the Father is in you? So, when I go I will never be so far off as even to be near, for nearness implies separation. If I go to the Father and I and my Father are one, where can I go? And when I come to you it will be to unfold myself, which is the pattern in you. Don't look for me to come as flesh and blood on the outside, but as the pattern unfolding from within! In the end all will awaken to be the one body, the one Lord, one hope, one faith, the one God and Father of all. Returning one by one, we are that one body, one Spirit, one Love!

Dwell upon my words for, in spite of all the turmoil in the world, we are all one. Thinking on the lowest level, men are trying to solve the problems of the world there, and it cannot be done. It's all done by repentance, by radical changes in attitudes of mind. A fact is confronted. All right, isn't it a fact that everything is possible to God? And if all things are possible to God and his name is "I am" can a fact not be changed? Can it not be resolved? At this very moment I can ignore the fact and assume things are as I want them to be, can I not? And when I assume, God is assuming, for his name and I are one. If all things are possible to God, are not all things possible to me? So if I have faith in God I must have faith in my imaginal acts. Faith in your imaginal acts turns you around and you will keep on turning around by practicing repentance, and as you do, you awake. Then you will find a group and tell them that if they will but turn around they will find God. That He's not coming from without but, pointing to your forehead, you will tell them He's all there. Then you will speak from experience, for as He unfolds himself within you, you will experience the perfect pattern my friend received with the four golden arrows. As I mentioned a few months ago, who knows what the awakened Man is doing when he shoots his arrows beyond the world of dream? You can't deviate from God's plan. If you awaken within yourself and it's the plan that awakens, you are the plan that awoke, so you shoot the plan to those you love.

Take the passages I have quoted tonight and see how they relate to the visions. Each passage dwells with eschatology, the doctrine of the last days, when Man turns from this age of sin and death to that age of Eternal life.

Now this may seem a deep spiritual night to many of you, but may I tell you it is directly practical, for while you were with me this night you left all of your worries and cares of the day on the conveyer belt which is moving automatically. Your heavenly Father knows your needs and is caring for them while you travel in the spirit world with me. You have left those who are self-complacent, content with their own little circle. Those who know they are right are in hell where there is no forgiveness of sin. In hell it's all self-righteousness, all justifying oneself. One of the greatest of all human weaknesses is the necessity of always being right, and that is hell until one becomes loose enough to ask questions. Whether the truth is accepted or not is irrelevant, but when they ask, answer directly: "When you find God you are going to find yourself. And when you find the truth you will discover that you and God the Father are one."

If you haven't read the beautiful 17th chapter of John, I urge you to do so. I think it is the most glorious prayer ever written. "O Father, I have manifested thy name to those thou gavest to me. They were yours and you gave them to me that they may be one even as we are one." Here he tells you that God and his pattern are one. In the beginning was the Word (the plan, the meaning of it all) and the Word was with God and the Word was God. So the pattern and he who sent it are one. The pattern is what was sent.

Always claiming that he was sent, he tells you that the sender (the Father) and the sent (the pattern) are one; therefore, the Father sends himself as the pattern which unfolds. Then the man in whom it unfolds tells it, and he always has a remnant who hears and believes. He won't get the world to believe him, for they are busy moving down on the conveyer belt. Although they hear the call to repent, they will not stop to change their beliefs for one little moment.

I have an aunt, now in her nineties. She was born and raised in a group called "The Brothers", the most bigoted Christian organization there ever was. One day while visiting her, I said: "Don't you know that the Bible teaches that Jesus had brothers?" Well, she almost slapped me in the face as she denied it. She attends church seven days a week, yet when I opened the Bible to the 6th chapter of Mark and read it to her she would not change her thinking relative to Christ. Unwilling to accept a foreign thought, she chooses to remain on the conveyer belt. Her mind is made up and she is not willing to read the Bible with a different understanding.

She will eventually die, to find herself restored to life in a world just like this, with a body the same as before only young with nothing missing - and she will not even realize what took place. She will still have the same fixed beliefs and she'll go through another pattern of events to become proximate matter - matter that is made to receive a form, like taking a piece of wax and making it soft enough to receive a seal.

In the 1st chapter of Hebrews, we are told that Jesus is the express image of his Father. He is not someone that looks like his Father, but is identical, like the imprinting of a seal on wax. My friend saw proximate matter in the skull. She saw that which is being molded and shaped and made more pliable to receive the impression.

Now let us go into the silence.

# Eternal States

S it quietly and ask yourself who you are, where you are and what you are. Your answers will reveal your state of consciousness: your body of belief. Paul said, "We do not look to the outer things, but to the things unseen, for the outer things are transient, but the unseen things are eternal." Your beliefs, seen by the mystic, are personified. They form a state, which completely controls your behavior. Any modification within your body of belief will result in a change in your outer world.

Blake tells us, "Eternity exists and all things in eternity independent of creation which was an act of mercy. By this you will see that I do not consider either the just or the wicked to be in a supreme state, but to be everyone of them states of the sleep which the soul may fall into in its deadly dreams of good and evil when it leaves paradise following the serpent."

Now, Blake uses the word "mercy" only as one who sees that states are eternal; that in God's mercy he created all things, not just a few, so that any situation which can be conceived, already exists in eternity. When Blake said, "Eternity exists and all things in eternity independent of creation which was an act of mercy," he meant that everything you see is dead, a part of the eternal structure of the universe. You are its operant power. When you enter a scene it becomes animated. Then you become lost in your own animation and think it is independent of your perception. Looking at it, you cannot believe you are causing the animation, but you are.

You and I are living souls, buried in a world of death. We are destined to be life-giving spirits through an act of mercy, but until that time we animate what we perceive. Questioning self, Blake asks: "O miserable man that I am, who will deliver me from this body of death?" May I tell you, no earthly power can do it, only God.

Peter tells us, "Blessed be the God and Father of the Lord Jesus Christ. By his great mercy we have been born anew to a living hope through the resurrection of Jesus Christ from the dead." This is true, for only by God's act of great mercy can we be born anew. Now buried in a world of eternal death, you are animating dead forms, believing they are independent of your perception of them. This you will continue to do until God's great mercy awakens Jesus Christ within you. If Christ was not buried in you, he could not awaken in you, and if he is not in you he could not emerge from you. Therefore, like Paul, you carry in your body the death of Jesus. It is the tomb in which he is buried. His awakening delivers you from a body of death, but until that time you must live in, and adjust to, the dead body you wear.

Now, until you are born from above, you operate the power which gives life to this world. For the world is a dream filled with dead scenery, while you are Proteus. As you enter the scene you cause the parts to be made alive. Not knowing this, you think there are others, and fight the shadows of your own being.

All things exist in the human imagination, and all phenomena are solely produced by imagining. Where there is no imagining, everything vanishes. If lack is now in your world, and you cease to be aware of it by imagining plenty, lack disappears; therefore, any modification in your body of belief will cause a change in your life.

Now embedded in death, we resurrect into life by the act of mercy. Scripture calls this transformation Jesus Christ, for it is he who is buried in us; and when he awakens and rises, we are born from above, thereby setting us free from this body of death. Until that moment in time you can enter a state, partake of it and move on to another. This is how it is done. Although I am living here in Los Angeles, I desire to be in New York City. While lying on my bed tonight, I close my physical eyes to the room surrounding me and assume I am in New York City. Then I ask myself these questions: If I were now in New York City, what would I see? Would I think of Los Angeles as three thousand miles to the west of me? Where are my friends and loved ones? How are my finances now that I am here? Then I would answer these questions carefully and fall asleep in New York City.

Now, an assumption is an act of faith, and without faith it is impossible to please God. "By faith we understand that the world was created by the word of God, so that things seen were made out of things that do not appear." Someone looking at my physical body would see me sleeping in Los Angeles, yet I would be sleeping in New York City, for I am all imagination and must be where I am imagining myself to be. By this action I am adjusting myself imaginatively to a state I desire to objectively realize. And if I have imagined with conviction, by giving New York City all of the sensory vividness of reality, things will immediately begin to happen to compel me to make the journey. I do not imagine lightly anymore, because I now know every imaginal act will come to pass.

When I first stumbled upon this principle, I thought it was stupid. The idea that imagining creates reality was nonsense. How could anyone believe a thing into being without any external evidence to support it? How could any imaginal act be the causative fact, which fuses and projects itself? Although I did not believe it could, I imagined, and got that which I did not want! So I acquaint you now with what I know about this principle of imagining and lead you to your choice and its risk. There is always a risk, for you may not want what you have imagined after you get it, so I warn you to select wisely.

Do you know what you want from life? You can be anything you want to be if you know who you are. Start from the premise, "I am all imagination and pass through states," for eternity, all things exist now! Having experienced a state and moved into another one you may think the former state has ceased to be, but all states are eternal, they remain forever. Like the mental traveler that you are, you pass through states either wittingly or unwittingly, but your individual identity is forever. Whether you are rich or poor, you retain the same individual identity when you move from one state into another. If you are not on guard, you can be persuaded by the press, television, or radio, to change your concept of self and unwittingly move into an undesirable state. You can move into many states and play many parts, but as the actor, you do not change your identity. When you are rich, you are the same actor as when you are poor. These are only different parts you are playing.

You annexed your physical body for the experiences you are now having, but you are not the body you wear. The day will come when you will awaken to this fact. Then, like Proteus, you will assume any shape for the part you want to play. If it takes a fish, you will be a fish. If it takes a man, you will be a man, for that is who God is. Learn to adjust your senses to what you desire to be. Just as I moved to New York City, you can move into the state of wealth, fame, or any state you desire.

Determine what it would feel like, and adjust your thinking by assuming you are feeling it now.

Look at your world mentally. Your present level of objective fact may be the same as it was before, but in your imagination hear your friends congratulate you on your good fortune. Then believe in the reality of this unseen experience. Like Paul, look not to things seen, but to things unseen; for the things seen are temporal, while the things unseen are eternal. Two hundred years ago Blake made the statement, "Eternity exists and all things in eternity, independent of creation which was an act of mercy." Three thousand years ago the unknown writer of Ecclesiastes said it even more beautifully: "There is nothing new under the sun. Is there a thing for which it is said, 'This is new?' It has been already in ages past, but there is no remembrance of things to come after, among those who will come later."

This past year one of our great physicists, Professor Richard Feynman of Cal Tech, said the same thing, yet not as beautifully as Blake or the unknown author of Ecclesiastes. This is what Professor Feynman said: "The entire space/time history of the world is laid out and we only become aware of increasing portions of it successively." For this Professor Feynman received the Nobel Prize and maybe $50,000, while Blake, who saw it mystically and recorded it poetically, went to an unmarked pauper's grave. Professor Feynman based his conclusion on his study of the disintegration of the atom. Noticing the peculiar behavior of a little positron when placed in fluid, he realized that the entire space/ time history of the world is already laid out, and man only becomes aware of portions of it successively.

I have seen the same thing in vision and know that the world is dead. I have entered a room such as this, to discover that I am the spirit animating it. By arresting the activity in me that caused the scene to become alive, everything froze. The waitress walked not. The birds flew not. The diners dined not. Then I knew that when I released its activity in me, everything and everyone would continue to complete their intention. Releasing my power, the waitress completed the serving, the bird flew to the limb of the tree, and the grass began to wave, as the leaf which was arrested in space fell to the ground. Now I know I am the center of creative power. The day will come when you, too will awaken and exercise your creative power, knowingly. That is our destiny, for we all will awaken as God and use this power to create in the true sense of the word.

Try to remember that there is no limit to God's creative power, or your power of belief. Persuade yourself that things are as you desire them to be. Fall asleep in that assumption, as that is your act of faith. Tomorrow the world will begin to change, to make room for the garment of your assumption. If it takes one person or ten thousand to aid the birth of your assumption, they will come. You will not need their consent or permission, because the world is dead and what would be the purpose in asking dead people to help you? Simply know what you want, animate the scene and those playing their parts will begin to move towards the fulfillment of your desire.

Try it before you pass judgment upon it. I know it doesn't make sense, but it will prove itself in performance and then it will not matter what the world thinks. If there is evidence for a thing, does it really matter what someone else thinks about it? I encourage you to try it, for if you do you will not fail.

Now let us go into the silence.

*Also Available from This Author*

| TITLE | ISBN |
|---|---|
| *Walk by Faith* | *9781603867474* |
| *Imagination Creates Reality* | *9781603867467* |
| *Come, O Blessed & Other Sermons* | *9781603867450* |
| *Behold the Dreamer Cometh and Other Sermons* | *9781603867443* |
| *An Assured Understanding & Other Sermons* | *9781603867436* |
| *A Divine Event and Other Essays* | *9781603867429* |
| *All Things Are Possible* | *9781603867405* |
| *Neville Goddard: The Essential Collection* | *9781603866781* |
| *At Your Command* | *9781603866774* |
| *You Can Never Outgrow I Am* | *9781603866767* |
| *The Secret of Imagining* | *9781603866750* |
| *Neville Goddard: The Complete Reader - Vol 1* | *9781603866743* |
| *Out of This World: Thinking Fourth-Dimensionally* | *9781603865647* |
| *Your Faith Is Your Fortune* | *9781603865593* |
| *Feeling is the Secret* | *9781603865449* |
| *Five Lessons* | *9781603865357* |
| *Three Propositions and Eleven Other Essays* | *9781603865296* |
| *The Power of Awareness* | *9781603865043* |
| *Awakened Imagination* | *9781603865036* |
| *Prayer: The Art of Believing* | *9781603864978* |
| *The Fourth Dimension* | *1603860266* |

www.ingramcontent.com/pod-product-compliance
Lightning Source LLC
Chambersburg PA
CBHW020604030426

42337CB00013B/1207